SCANDALS

Stories of Sex, Intrigue and Corruption

LONGMEADOW
PRESS

Copyright © Bookmart Ltd/Amazon Publishing 1992
This book created for Bookmart by Amazon Publishing Ltd

This 1992 edition published by Longmeadow Press, 201 High Ridge Road, Stamford, CT 06904.

Cover design by Cooper Wilson

Thanks to the Hulton Picture Company and
Mary Evans Picture Library for sourcing pictures.

Library of Congress Cataloging-in-Publication Data is available upon request

ISBN 0-681-416451

Printed in Czechoslovakia

0 9 8 7 6 5 4 3 2 1

SCANDALS

IMELDA MARCOS
The Iron Butterfly

Rags-to-riches stories are not unusual. But the appallingly corrupt Imelda Marcos ruled the Filipino people with a rod of iron, ignoring their squalor and poverty while squandering the country's money on herself

To her few supporters Imelda Marcos was known as the mother of her country, a rags-to-riches beauty who overcame a limited education to fête and deal on equal terms with presidents, kings and popes.

But to her critics she was the violator of her country, a money-grabbing, despotic witch who indulged her every whim while her compatriots eked out a living in their ramshackle tin ghettos.

Imelda inspired great loyalty, but even greater hatred. As the wife of former Philippines President Ferdinand Marcos, and as his chief diplomat, executioner and loyalist, she has become a twentieth-century Marie Antoinette, despised and ridiculed as the Iron Butterfly.

Her greed, gluttony and selfishness knew no bounds. While her peasant 'worshippers' starved, her dog wore a

Above: *Imelda Marcos rouses her loyal followers with a song on her return to Manila in November 1991. Behind her is her son Ferdinand Marcos Junior.*

Opposite: *A military band plays for Imelda Marcos and a friend...she was demure, sophisticated, beautiful, adored and despised as the female despot of the Far East.*

Left: *President and Mrs Marcos on a state visit to Japan drink a toast to Prime Minister Eisaku Sato in Tokyo in 1966. Marcos was a war hero following his campaigns against the Japanese.*

diamond necklace. While her nation struggled to meet its foreign debts, she spent her country's treasury on everything from Bulgari baubles to pastel-coloured mink coats.

Her supporters starved, but her dog wore a diamond collar

Visitors to the Malacanang Palace - now a museum - know first-hand of her all-consuming greed. Under Imelda's former sumptuous bedroom is a 5000 sq ft basement, where visitors can gasp at the now infamous monument to corruption: 2700 pairs of shoes, 500 black brassieres, 1500 handbags, 35 large racks stacked with fur coats and 1200 designer gowns she wore but once.

During shopping trips to Paris, Rome or New York she stayed at the plushest hotels, where there was a standing order to provide her rooms with £500 worth of fresh flowers every day.

After partying with wealthy jet-setters she would then resume her journeys in a private twin-engined plane complete with built-in shower and gold bathroom fixtures. And through it all, she scoffed at the critics. 'The poor people want me to be their star,' she would sniff.

But these lavish spending sprees were

*Above: **An idol in her own land, Mrs Marcos views a statue in Cairo museum during a visit to Egypt.***

*Below: **President Marcos in 1971 at the time of yet another armed insurrection in the Philippines. Martial law cemented the power base of the Marcos dynasty.***

but a pittance compared with her major crimes. She reportedly stole - with the help of her husband - some $5 billion from the Philippine treasury.

SCALING THE SOCIAL LADDER

But her early days were spent in poverty, not luxury. Imelda Romualdez was a poor, barefoot child whose family lost almost all its valuable possessions when the Japanese occupied the Philippines in World War II. Those closest to her say it was her impoverished childhood that gave rise to her greed.

In spite of the poverty, however, the future first lady did have one thing going for her as a teenager. She was classically beautiful, a tall, wide-eyed 'Asian Angel'. Her stunning looks did not go unnoticed by the rising young senator Ferdinand Marcos, who quickly realized that his shrewdness and ambition, together with her charms, would make a politically irresistible combination.

He was right, and after their marriage in 1954 Imelda became a tireless campaign worker for him, often singing traditional Filipino folk songs to stir up the crowds before her husband addressed them. They were the most glamorous political duo the nation had seen.

But it was a hectic, grinding road to the Malacanang Palace. In later years Imelda would recall that the rigours of playing wife, mother, political aide and adviser became so much that she suffered a nervous breakdown. Marcos packed his wife off to New York for a break. Doctors there told her either to get used to the very public life of a politician's wife, or to leave him. She learned to handle it, then to embrace it.

Eventually the years of hard work and campaigning paid off. In 1965 Ferdinand Marcos was voted into the presidency. He and his wife would rule the country with an iron fist for the next twenty-one years.

At first, the Marcoses had to pay some regard to the Philippine constitution. But after eight years Ferdinand knew he could not run for a third term under the existing laws. So, on 21 September 1972, he declared martial law.

Irksome things like elections, due process of law and freedom of the press could now be done away with. But not the growing resentment of the people.

Just two months after the declaration of martial law, Imelda was officiating at an awards ceremony when one of the recipients suddenly lunged at her with a long, curved knife known as a *bolo*.

Imelda never threw away any article of clothing - to prevent it being seized for use in voodoo rituals against her

---

Her attacker was quickly killed by palace security guards, but not before he had badly slashed her on both arms. From that day on, Imelda would always wear a scarf at her throat in heed of a soothsayer's warning that it would ward off a beheading. And never again did she throw away any personal article of clothing, lest it be used in voodoo rites to unleash evil spirits against her.

CHIEF DIPLOMAT

Although martial law cemented the Marcoses' power base, Ferdinand rarely left the palace. Instead he relied increasingly on his socially adroit wife to handle overseas diplomatic missions.

These she frequently turned into mass buying sprees with her infamous 'Blue Ladies' - socialite supporters. They wore white *ternos* - the traditional native Filipino dress with butterfly sleeves - with 'Marcos blue' sashes. Together, Imelda and her 'ladies in waiting' would tour the world, buying and partying their way through the 1970s.

Whenever she departed or landed at the capital, the whole of Manila airport was frozen to other air traffic, while hundreds of native-costumed children, friends, cabinet ministers, wives and military leaders were forced to see her off, or welcome her home.

Visiting dignitaries were also afforded these garish displays - though one, in 1981, was a petty, tasteless joke at the expense of the Pope.

Years before, when Imelda was visiting Rome, she had been granted an audience with the Holy Father and insisted on wearing a white *terno*. Vatican protocol officials politely

Below: *Imelda Marcos, dressed like royalty, goes shopping during a visit to London in 1970.*

informed her that she must wear black, with long sleeves. Eventually Imelda was resigned to wearing black, but she never forgot the 'insult'. So when Pope John

*Above: **President Marcos the world statesman, fêted by Western leaders while his police and soldiers quelled unrest at home with the threat of the gun. He took a model democracy to a total dictatorship.***

*Left: **A garlanded President Ferdinand Marcos has a quiet word in the ear of UN Secretary - General Kurt Waldheim during an economic conference in Kenya in 1976.***

Paul II arrived in Manila, every one of the hundreds of 'Blue Ladies' was instructed to greet him bare-armed in white *ternos*.

The Pope wasn't the only VIP to bear the brunt of Imelda's vindictiveness. Years earlier, the Beatles had learned first hand of her brutishness. When the famed pop group were touring the Philippines in 1966 Mrs Marcos let it be known that she would like them to play for her at the Malacanang Palace.

The Fab Four sent back word that if she wanted to see them she could come to their stadium concert. The snub infuriated the egotistical Iron Butterfly, and on the day the band left Manila they were attacked by some of her hired thugs.

The 'Blue Ladies' also helped Imelda in organizing the lavish parties she threw - including her own birthday bash every July. That 'national celebration' was often held at the beachside palace at Olot, which contained two Olympic-size swimming pools, an eighteen-hole golf course and three heliports.

One of her favorite pastimes at Olot was to serenade guests in her soprano voice - her 'repertoire' ranged from folk ballads to Western pop tunes. Sometimes even Ferdinand would join her, and together they would sing a love ballad.

After a perceived snub by the Beatles, Imelda had them beaten up at Manila airport

---

Visitors were also given mementoes of their stays - usually gems or gold. Underneath her palace Imelda had store rooms filled with such 'trinkets'.

A compulsive, obsessive shopper, Imelda would buy a dozen pairs of the same shoes if she liked them, and hundreds of the same blouse. In one trip, a 1983 jaunt through Rome, Copenhagen and New York, she splurged more than £3 million in just ninety days. The tab included everything from £2 million for a Michelangelo painting to £8000 pounds for bath towels!

And always she scoffed at suggestions that she and her husband were corrupt. 'They call me corrupt, frivolous,' she complained. 'I would not look like this if I am corrupt. Some ugliness would settle down on my system.'

SANDS FROM AUSTRALIA

But Imelda didn't have to travel, of course, to spend her spare change. While preparing to play hostess to European royals and dignitaries at the 1979 opening of the Marbella beach resort outside Manila, she noticed that the sand wasn't white enough. So she simply sent a plane to Australia for a load of sand of the correct colour.

According to those who knew her, Imelda's buying binges and ruthless quest for power started in 1969 - after she learned

her husband was having an affair with an American actress, Dovie Beams. She immediately sent the woman back to the USA. But Beams had secretly recorded her lovemaking sessions with the President.

On one buying binge she bought a Michelangelo painting and £8000 worth of bath towels

---

Copies of those tapes fell into the hands of the Marcoses' political enemies including Senator Ninoy Aquino, who often joked about their contents. That began Imelda's intense hatred of the senator, who was jailed in 1972.

Publicly humiliated by her husband's infidelity - and Beams's statements that Ferdinand thought Imelda frigid - she gave the President an ultimatum. She would not seek a divorce, and she would still campaign for him - but at a price. The price was that he would not interfere with her grandiose schemes to put the Philippines on the world map.

These extraordinary plans included the Manila Film Festival. It folded after just two years - but not before it had proved how callous Imelda could be. As construction on the huge building to house the festival fell behind schedule, corners were cut. Cement floors were not allowed to dry properly before the next phase of construction began. Inevitably, there was a disaster - a floor collapsed and killed up to 168 workers.

Relatives came to collect the bodies, but before they could claim them the order came down that not even a national tragedy could delay construction. The dead were covered by cement.

By 1975, the President had lost all control of his wife. She had him appoint her to top government positions, and flaunted her friendships with handsome jet-set cronies.

Imelda made a deal with the unfaithful President: she would still support him provided he let her lust for power and possessions go unchecked

---

But those who knew her believe the relationships were not of a sexual nature. The icy Imelda liked her men for public display, not private pleasures.

By 1979 she had become so powerful that she launched a cabinet shake-up, and

Above: *Mr and Mrs Marcos receive gifts on a state visit. Normally her presents were more beautiful than mere flowers. She once said: 'They call me corrupt. I would not look like this if I am corrupt.'*

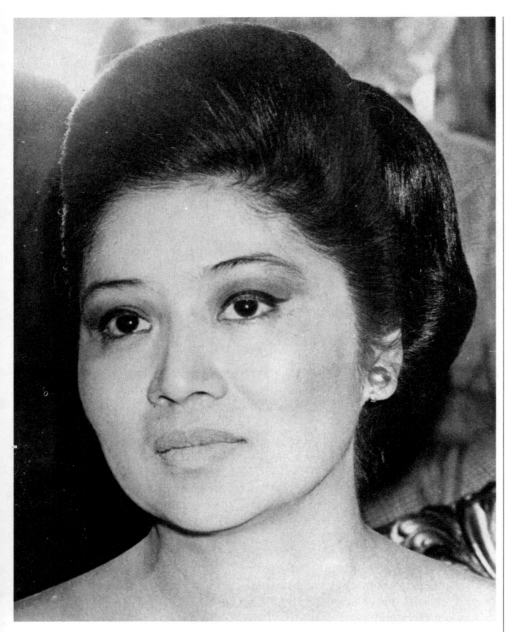

It came as no surprise to anyone when he was proclaimed the people's choice! The few opponents who challenged the dictatorial couple were quickly quashed.

Now, firmly cemented in power once again, the First Lady decided to do some real buying - this time expensive real estate in New York. She snapped up properties like designer dresses - the Herald Centre shopping complex, the prestigious Crown Building on plush Fifth Avenue, office complexes on Wall Street and Madison Avenue, homes in New Jersey and New York's Long Island.

As Ferdinand's health deteriorated, she meddled more and more in affairs of state. But events were developing which would make her manoeuvring worthless.

THE BEGINNING OF THE END

In August 1983 Ninoy Aquino, who had been in exile in the United States for several years, returned to the Philippines. As he stepped off the plane he was shot dead, the victim of a plot by one of the Marcoses' cronies.

The Marcos regime scrambled to control the damage, but it would never overcome the ensuing turmoil and cries for justice. The Aquino murder was the last straw for many who previously had been too scared or too ignorant to care.

Now there were daily demonstrations, the media grew bolder, workers went on strike and there were even cries for Ferdinand's impeachment.

But the President was by this time gravely ill from a series of ailments. Imelda knew their grip on the country was weakening, and she turned for reassurance to occultists and soothsayers.

With the Marcoses' grip on the country slipping fast, Imelda turned to occultists and soothsayers for reassurance

---

The regime was also coming under increasing pressure from the USA - long its staunchest and most generous ally. So in 1986, somehow believing he could ensure another four years in power, Ferdinand called a snap election.

But the years of brutality had finally caught up on the First Couple. Corazon

the presidential ministers became known as 'Imelda's Cabinet'. Family members and cronies were placed in senior positions, and profitable businesses were 'miraculously' transferred to those who pleased her.

In 1981 the President suspended martial law and put himself up for re-election - but all opposition was rapidly put down

---

But even Ferdinand realized that he and his wife could not maintain absolute power indefinitely under martial law. In 1981 he put himself up for re-election.

Above: *Arrogant beyond belief, by 1975 the President had lost all control over his power-hungry wife. He appointed her to a high government office.*

Aquino, the widow of Senator Aquino, was swept to power. On 15 February, despite evidence of nationwide rigging, Ferdinand declared himself the winner.

The Philippines plunged into near revolution, and Ferdinand and Imelda finally fled one night taking whatever booty they could.

EXILE...AND RETURN

Ferdinand, racked by illness, died in their Hawaiian exile less than three years later, leaving Imelda to face the complex array of court cases against her family for their two-decade orgy of greed and corruption.

But tracking down the millions in foreign banks and property holdings in New York, Rome and London and elsewhere may prove too difficult for even the most dedicated detectives.

American officials say they are not sure how much money she might be worth, but it could be as much as £7.5 billion. Whether any will eventually be returned to the people of the Philippines is impossible to say, but under a New York court ruling in 1990 Imelda was allowed to keep all her money and investments in America.

Incredibly, she believes she is being persecuted by ungrateful compatriots and that she and her husband 'worked hard to be the symbol of what each and every Filipino would like to fight and die for: freedom, justice, democracy and, above all, human dignity'.

In 1990 the former First Lady was allowed to return home - on condition that she would face tax charges.

Imelda still belives that during their rule she and Ferdinand stood for freedom, justice, democracy and human dignity

---

Astonishingly, she has ended up running for the presidency. 'Whatever the people want from me, I shall obey,' she had said before leaving for home. It seems that the people - by her reckoning at least - have called on her to put her name forward as a contender to succeed Corazon Aquino in the 1991 elections.

Below: *Part of Imelda Marcos's collection of shoes. She was a shopaholic. In just 90 days of a shopping spree through New York, Rome and Copenhagen she splurged more than £3 million.*

WATERGATE
A Presidential Scandal

When an alert security guard reported a break-in he unwittingly exposed a tale of immorality, subversion and political scandal. The break-in took place in Washington's exclusive Watergate complex, and its ultimate victim was President Nixon himself

Above: *'Freshmen' Congressmen line up after winning election to the US House of Representatives in 1947. Richard Nixon stands on the far right in the back row alongside John F. Kennedy.*

Opposite: *World War I hero Dwight D. Eisenhower's vice-presidential running mate Richard Nixon, during the 1952 election campaign.*

Right: *A stern-looking President Gerald Ford, Nixon's successor, in the Oval office with the veteran Secretary of State Henry Kissinger.*

It was a little after two o'clock on the morning of Saturday, 17 June 1972. Five men, dressed in dark business suits and wearing rubber surgical gloves, made their way quietly through the maze of blackened offices and corridors, their vast array of hi-tech equipment in tow.

Despite their obvious professionalism and knowledge of the layout, they could not have foreseen that an alert security guard would, at that moment, decide to make his rounds of the complex.

The arrest of five burglars would normally be an inside page story in the local paper. This time it would be headlines worldwide

---

Realizing there had been a break-in, the guard immediately called the Washington Police Department which sent a squad car to the scene. The five men, found cowering in one of the vacant offices, were arrested and held for arraignment.

Six hours later, the phone rang in reporter Bob Woodward's one-room apartment. The young ex-Naval officer fumbled for the phone, to hear the city editor at the *Washington Post* order him down to the courthouse.

Woodward wasn't impressed at first with his Saturday assignment - the arrest of five burglars. Nevertheless, his interest peaked somewhat when told that the burglary had occurred at the headquarters of the Democrat National Committee.

And so began the most explosive story in American political history - a scandal that would climax with the fall of President Richard Milhouse Nixon.

After its course had run, the very name 'Watergate' would be synonymous with immorality, subversion and officially sanctioned crimes.

Above: *Republican candidate Richard Nixon was given a tumultuous reception in 1960 when he took the stage with President Eisenhower and Mr Cabot Lodge.*

THE RISE TO POWER

But Nixon's scandalous behaviour did not begin with Watergate. That was merely the culmination of a political life steeped in often shady conduct.

Curiously, the man who later wanted to hire union thugs to deal with anti-Vietnam activists began life as a Quaker, imbued with non-violent ideals. The second of five brothers, he was born on 9 January 1913 in the Californian town of Yorba Linda, where his father grew lemons. His parents were ordinary working people.

The man who sent thousands of young Americans to their deaths in Vietnam was actually born a Quaker

---

Although a shy, introverted youth, Nixon was nevertheless an excellent student. While he did well at all subjects, he preferred history and music. In a bid to overcome his inherent shyness he also took up public speaking, and became a leading member of college debating teams.

While working his way through Whittier College, a Quaker institution not far from where he was raised, he won a scholarship to the prestigious Duke University in North Carolina. In 1934, he entered law school there.

Three years later he emerged with his degree - third in his class - and joined a legal firm back in his home state of California. One of his outside activities was acting in an amateur theatre group, and it was there that he met pretty Pat Ryan, a red-haired typing teacher who would later become his wife.

Nixon became the aggressive mouthpiece of the 'Reds under the bed' paranoia that swept America after World War II

After the Japanese attack on Pearl Harbor on 7 December 1941 Nixon decided to do his part for the American war effort. So he moved to Washington, where he did legal work for the government. Later, despite his Quaker background, he was given a Navy commission as a lieutenant. He ended the war a lieutenant commander.

In 1946, on the urging of a banker friend, he decided to enter politics, running as a Republican in California's 12th congressional district.

The thirty-three-year-old Nixon won the seat easily, and within the next two years consolidated his position as a tough, no-nonsense politician.

In his second term in Congress he was

appointed to the controversial House of Un-American Activities Committee. Here his ruthlessness singled him out as the 'pit bull' of Congress, constantly badgering the American people with the deviousness of the Red mind.

His reputation as a Communist-hunter helped carry him to victory in the 1950 Senate race. He was now thirty-seven, and a veteran of Washington's wheeling-and-dealing machinations. Two years after becoming the youngest Republican senator he was selected by Dwight D. Eisenhower as his vice-presidential choice on the 1952 party ticket.

But in September Nixon's surging political life was almost cut down. He was nearly forced to quit the ticket after a New York newspaper accused him of secretly misusing £10,000 of campaign funds for his personal expenses.

Eisenhower told Nixon he would have to prove he was 'as clean as a hound's tooth' or face political exile

---

The outcry shook the Republican party, and Eisenhower told Nixon he would have to prove he was 'as clean as a hound's tooth' or face political exile.

On 23 September, the young senator appeared on national television, his wife at his side, to explain the alleged misconduct. His defence became known as the 'Checkers Speech'.

Nixon explained that the funds had been used entirely for political campaign purposes, and that he would never allow anything immoral or illegal to taint his career. Then he told his audience that although someone had given his children a dog - a cocker spaniel they named Checkers - he didn't believe he should take it away from them just because he was in the public eye.

He concluded the speech with a line that he would paraphrase more than twenty years later during Watergate: 'I don't believe I ought to quit, because I'm not a quitter.'

The American people believed in his innocence in overwhelming numbers, and he returned to what he did best - attacking his Democrat opponents. He claimed that the Democratic nominee for

*Above: **President Nixon was received by Pope Paul VI in a special audience at the Vatican. His piety was questioned in 1952 when the press accused him of misusing £10,000 of election campaign funds.***

*Left: **'Happy Birthday Mr President.' A king-sized birthday card from his White House staff is presented to Nixon by two secretaries on 9 January 1970.***

President, Adlai Stevenson, had given support to Alger Hiss. Hiss was a former State Department official whom Nixon had convicted as a Communist several years earlier.

The attacks duly paid off, and the Eisenhower-Nixon ticket steamrollered to a landslide victory.

AIMING AT THE WHITE HOUSE

With the retirement of Eisenhower, Nixon decided to aim for the top: the presidency. On his first attempt however, in 1960, he lost to the charismatic John F. Kennedy, and retired to California where he joined a law firm in Los Angeles.

But the power-hungry politician inside him would not stay idle long. Just eleven months after his narrow loss to Kennedy, he announced he would run for the governorship of California. This time he lost badly, and the wounded Nixon bitterly complained that the media had done him in with its 'biased' coverage. He solemnly announced he was quitting public life.

'You won't have Richard Nixon to kick around any more,' he stormed, and that was the last everyone thought they would hear of Richard Milhouse Nixon.

Two political failures in one year was too much for Nixon's pride, and he announced his retirement from public life

---

They were wrong. By 1968, six years after Nixon went into political 'retirement', America was a country at war with itself. The lengthy conflict in Vietnam had become a quagmire for the American military machine, and race riots were rocking the inner-city ghettos.

On top of that, President Johnson announced that he would not seek the Democratic Party's nomination for another term. This made the 1968 presidential race the most open in many years. That was enough incentive for Nixon. He quickly

Above: *Nixon the peace-maker. The President attends a conference in Moscow in 1972. His diplomatic efforts caused his popularity to soar.*

Below: *Edward Heath watches as Nixon shakes hands with the Queen at Chequers during his visit to Britain and Ireland in 1970.*

proved he could still be a vote-getter. With his running mate Spiro Agnew, the former Governor of Maryland, Nixon slipped into the White House with the slimmest of majorities - his margin of victory was 1/2 per cent.

The fifty-six-year-old Nixon had at last captured the highest office in the land. At the same time, the seeds of what would become known as Watergate were already being planted, thanks to his obsessive secrecy and distrust of anyone he feared might challenge his authority.

After winning the presidency with the slimmest of majorities, Nixon quickly turned it into a den of corruption

---

Although details would not surface until the early months of Nixon's second term, which began with a landslide victory in 1972, there were two major scandals brewing during his first four years. These were the Air Force bombing of Cambodia, and Watergate.

In 1970, as the Vietnam War dragged on, Nixon assured the American people that Cambodia's neutrality would be respected by the United States. Later, it was learned that the USA had carried out more than 3500 bombing sorties over Cambodia in 1969-70.

But this gruesome deception would later pale into insignificance once the full extent of Nixon's immorality - and that of 'all the President's men' - became known through Watergate.

THE WATERGATE AFFAIR

After the 1972 break-in and arraignment of the five burglars a massive cover-up operation began inside the White House. Thanks, however, to the dogged efforts of people like reporter Bob Woodward and his colleague Carl Bernstein, the world eventually learned the truth.

But as early as 1969 there was a hint of what was to come when John Mitchell, then Attorney-General, claimed that presidential powers permitted the use of wiretapping without court supervision.

A second clue - though no one outside the administration could have known - came in July 1970, when Nixon approved the intelligence community's plan to subvert his domestic opponents through break-ins and covert mail coverage.

There were, of course, many behind-the-scenes instances of Nixon's lust for power. As revealed in the White House tapes several years later, Nixon suggested using hired thugs from the Mafia-controlled Teamsters' Union to break up

Top: *Nixon on his inauguration day in January 1969 when he became 37th President of the United States...and the face of disgrace in 1974.*

Above: *Former White House aide John Dean testifies before the Senate committee investigating the Watergate scandal in Washington in 1973. The evidence increasingly damned the President.*

anti-war demonstrations. 'They've got guys who'll go in and knock their heads off,' was Nixon's gleeful comment.

And before the election he wanted the tax records of insufficiently loyal bureaucrats. When asked by his aides how they would obtain these details from inside the Internal Revenue Service building, Nixon replied: 'Goddamn it! Sneak in in the middle of the night.'

The President was so paranoid about plots against him that he set up a secret investigations unit known as the 'plumbers'

But the first real Watergate-related incident came in the wake of the release of the so-called Pentagon Papers in 1971.

Even though these documents, which were leaked to the *New York Times*, detailed the secret history of previous administrations' policies in Vietnam, Nixon was sure it was part of a plot against his own administration. To

safeguard against further releases he set up a secret special investigations unit.

The unit, known as the 'plumbers', included senior adviser John Ehrlichman, Egil Krough, Gordon Liddy, Howard Hunt and David Young. All would later gain infamy in the Watergate scandal.

One of Ehrlichman's first tasks was to draw up a 'Priority List' of twenty of the President's 'political enemies'. At the top of that list was Senator Edward Kennedy. The unit also discussed the possible killing of crusading newspaper columnist Jack Anderson and the sabotage of Democratic rallies.

Nixon and his aides had persuaded themselves that the US intelligence set-up was their own personal spy network

---

By the time the full extent of the Watergate scandal became known, the word 'Watergate' had long since meant more than an office break-in.

As the investigation neared its dramatic conclusions in 1974, the affair had brought down two Attorney-Generals, most of the senior White House staff and Vice President Agnew, who had abused his office to accept 'kickbacks'.

As if that were not enough, it was eventually uncovered that Nixon had

Above: *Thumbs up...but the road was all downhill in August 1974 as Richard Nixon, with son-in-law David Eisenhower, bids farewell to his White House staff.*

Above right: *Nixon hugs his daughter Julie in his private quarters at the White House after the heart-wrenching decision to resign as President of the United States.*

been telling bare-faced lies to the American people when he reassured them that he had no knowledge of the break-in.

WORTHY OF IMPEACHMENT

'I am not a crook,' he said during one televised speech. But the records and tapes indicated otherwise, and moves were mounting to have him impeached. In fact, the Justice Committee of the House of Representatives had already recommended impeachment.

Its report was a stinging indictment of a President who had run amok. It read that Richard Nixon 'has acted in a manner contrary to his trust as President and subversive of constitutional government...such conduct warrants impeachment and trial, and removal from office'. Despite those strong words Nixon still refused to yield his office, telling the nation: 'I have no intention whatever of ever walking away from the job that the American people elected me to do...'

However, the Watergate steamroller could not be stopped.

On 16 July 1973, White House aide Alexander Butterfield disclosed that since 1970 Nixon had secretly recorded all conversations and phone calls in his offices. Congress demanded that the tapes be handed over. But Nixon 'hunkered down', to use a favourite expression, and refused to yield the tapes, claiming 'executive privilege'.

Eventually, realizing he had no choice, Nixon offered to hand over summary transcripts of the tapes. Archibald Cox, the special prosecutor who had been appointed by the Justice Department to co-ordinate the Watergate probes, took issue with Nixon's partial compliance.

The tapes would eventually reveal him as a foul-mouthed vindictive man who had abused the trust of the American people

---

But by this time Nixon's gall knew no limits, and in the infamous 'Saturday Night Massacre' of 20 October Cox was fired by the President's hand-picked Attorney-General, Robert Bork.

It was clear to everyone, however, that Nixon was fighting a losing battle. The tapes would eventually reveal him to be a foul-mouthed, vindictive man.

By late February, the Watergate prosecution team had obtained guilty pleas to a variety of criminal enterprises from a host of former Nixon associates. In addition, irregularities were found in the President's tax returns. It was also disclosed that he had used about £10 million of government money to improve his homes in Florida and California.

By June 1974, Nixon had become a virtual prisoner inside the White House.

The next month, John Ehrlichman and other White House 'plumbers' were found guilty of conspiracy, and twelve days later the Supreme Court ruled unanimously that Nixon had no choice but to turn over sixty-four missing tapes.

THE END OF A PRESIDENT

The end came, finally, on 9 August. Knowing that he was now certain to be impeached by Congress, Nixon resigned the presidency in an emotional farewell address. Then he retreated to his home in California - a bitter, broken man.

Yet, thanks to that great healer, time, Richard Nixon is today considered by many to have been a first-rate world statesman. In effect, his renaissance began less than a month after his exit

from Washington, when his hand-picked successor, Gerald Ford, pardoned him of all criminal doings while in office.

In the years since, Nixon has tried to play down the horrors of Watergate. He prefers to say that, in hindsight, he should have acted more quickly to defuse the situation. He recalled:

Looking back on what is still in my mind a complex and confusing mass of events, decisions, pressures and personalities, one thing I can see clearly now is that I was wrong in not acting more decisively and more forthrightly in dealing with Watergate... I know that many fair-minded people believe that my motivation and actions in the Watergate affair were intentionally self-serving and illegal. I now understand how my own mistakes and misjudgements have contributed to that belief...

Nixon, who was revealed as both liar and cheat for the entire world to see, still cannot bring himself to admit that it was he who was to blame.

Below: *In 1978 an older and wiser Richard Nixon visited Britain. He gave a welcoming smile to pressmen at London airport four years after he ceased to be US President.*

JEAN HARRIS
Scarsdale Diet Murderer

The Scarsdale Diet caused a sensation. But it was nothing compared with the story of its creator, Herman Tarnower. What turned a demure headmistress into his lover and then his murderer?

It ranks as one of the most sensational murder trials in contemporary American history and its outcome still leaves rancour and bitterness. When Jean Harris - spurned mistress of the famed Scarsdale Diet doctor Herman Tarnower - ended his cheating life with a gun, she unleashed a story of passion and jealousy that no fiction writer could ever have competed with. It was all there, a tabloid heaven of sex, intrigue, wealth, power, glamour, kinky games and murder.

What could have possessed a matronly, balanced woman in her fifties to plunge over the abyss into madness and kill a man hailed as a waistline messiah for millions of over-eaters? Did she intend to kill him or kill herself, as she told the jury at her trial? Does she deserve to languish in jail to this day?

In this case it was intent that was really on trial, for Jean Harris was a one-time killer who really ended her own love-lorn life when she shot Herman Tarnower.

THE VICTIM

Tarnower was born on 18 March 1910 in Brooklyn, New York, the son of a wealthy hat manufacturer. His early years were mirror images of the style he later came to enjoy so much. While many in impoverished Brooklyn lived hand-to-mouth existences, there were no such privations for the young Herman and his brothers and sisters.

He was bright and preferred to spend his adolescence reading the classics and

Opposite: *Jean Harris the high-powered girls' school headmistress was also an anguished lover aching for the security of marriage.*

Below: *The book that made Herman Tarnower's fortune* **The Scarsdale Diet,** *published in 1979 told would-be slimmers how to lose weight without giving up the good life.*

science books rather than in pool halls or at the beach. By the time he was seventeen he was over six feet tall and had acquired the nickname 'Hi'.

College was a cakewalk for him. At Syracuse College in New York State he always achieved grade As. He went on to medical school, and in 1933 graduated with his medical degree.

It was the depths of the Depression and some colleagues of his father's had already ended their lives as their fortunes crumbled. Tarnower knew that the world always needed doctors. He enrolled as an intern at New York's Bellevue Hospital.

Popping pills down his patients' throats, however, was not the way he wanted to continue life for ever. Medicine offered challenges he wished to explore in research laboratories. In 1936 he was awarded the Bowens Fellowship which

LOSE UP TO 20 POUNDS IN 14 DAYS AND KEEP THEM OFF

THE COMPLETE SCARSDALE MEDICAL DIET PLUS Dr. TARNOWER'S LIFETIME KEEP-SLIM PROGRAM

For the first time- the total plan for the diet that's taking America by storm, explained in full by the noted doctor who created it.

Herman Tarnower, M.D. & Samm Sinclair Baker

allowed him to travel for two years to England and Holland. He became particularly interested in heart disease as pioneers began to trace direct links between diet and disease.

When he returned to America it wasn't to New York but to the wealthy suburb of Scarsdale. He became a cardiologist, breaking new ground in the study of the heart and, while he was at it, making money hand over fist.

The ambitious Tarnower knew the world would always need doctors, Depression or not

---

He was a charming man described by writer Jay Davis: 'He made no bones about the fact that he was a man of very demanding appetites for the better things in life - and that included high cuisine, high art, high society. It also...included the society of beautiful, compelling, and willing women.'

The entry of America into World War II saw Dr Tarnower posted to hospital service with the American Army. When the atomic bombs were dropped on Japan he was invited to be part of the medical team which went into the shattered cities of Hiroshima and Nagasaki.

In peacetime he returned to Scarsdale, where a post-war baby boom and new prosperity brought many young couples to the area. It was also crammed with stressed-out executives whose hearts were going into overload.

In 1975 Tarnower penned the outline of what would eventually be published in 1979 as *The Scarsdale Diet*, the regimen for foodies who wanted to shed pounds but did not want to give up the gourmet delicacies they relished so much.

His mistress of fourteen years, Jean Harris, thought it was a great idea.

THE ACCUSED

Jean Harris - born Jean Struven - was a child of the Depression, but she was cushioned from its worst effects by the comfortable surroundings of her thrifty parents. She was the daughter of a military officer and her childhood and adolescence were spent in Cleveland,

Ohio, where she excelled at the best girls' schools in the area. She was at university during the war years, and graduated in 1945 with a degree in economics. A friend who remembers her said: 'She was a totally in-control person. A fine, wonderful girl and a born leader.'

In May 1946 Jean married James Harris, the son of a Michigan banking family. Her first son was born in 1950, her second four years later. But as the children grew up and her husband prospered, something stirred in her. She took a daring trip to Moscow in 1958, but returned even more unhappy and restless than before. She was plunged into depression when she failed to get a top teaching post at the school in their suburb of Detroit. Her frustrations culminated in her divorce from Harris in October 1964.

Jean went on to further education, gaining a master's degree in education before landing herself the job of director of the middle school at a girls' academy in Philadelphia. Here she met Dr Tarnower, who escorted her to the theatre, to restaurants and to his bed.

A dull marriage combined with professional frustration turned Jean Harris into a restless free spirit

---

It wasn't until 1972 that she moved to Connecticut and became the chief administrator of an exclusive girls' establishment called the Thomas School.

THE MURDER

That two people as refined, single and responsible as Herman Tarnower and Jean Harris should drift into each other's lives seems no big surprise.

But there was a sword of Damocles hanging over the relationship in the form of Tarnower's utter abhorrence of marriage. Poor Jean thought she was the woman to change him. 'It was', said one observer, 'the one dark shadow in her otherwise sunny life. She so desperately wanted to marry him and he so desperately wanted to remain single.'

In July 1977 she moved to Virginia to take over as the headmistress of another exclusive all-girl academy, Madeira

Opposite: Dr Herman Tarnower, cardiologist and philanderer. 'He made no bones about the fact that he was a man of very demanding appetites,' wrote one acquaintance.

Above: *Jean Harris and her lawyer Bonnie Steingart leave Westchester County Court.*

'Upstairs.'

'Who did it?'

'I did.'

As the body was taken away past her she yelled at him: 'Who was at dinner tonight? Who did you have here?' He died on the way to hospital.

THE TRIAL

Only when the demure divorcee was arraigned on the charge of murdering Dr Tarnower did the world glean the full extent of her passions. She pleaded not guilty to murder - claiming she went there with every intention of ending her own life that night, and that Tarnower died in a struggle that he instigated.

On the stand she painted a picture of years of emotional abuse at the hands of Tarnower - how she cooked and kept house for him, even though she knew he was taking his younger assistant Lynne out to dinner. She told how Hi - his nickname had become her pet name for him - boasted: 'I don't need love any more' as she begged him to marry her.

She revised chapters of his book *The Scarsdale Diet*, which made him wealthy, as he philandered with Lynne. She said: 'When his relationships with other women began to rub off on my life in ugly, dirty ways, my personal struggle over integrity became increasingly complicated. Should I walk away without flinching or stay without flinching?'

Soon the headlines began appearing in the tabloid papers in New York: 'Was Jean a Killer or a tragic victim?'

Just before his death Tarnower cut his fourteen-year lover out of his will in favour of her younger rival Lynne

---

Evidence poured out that Tarnower had instructed his housekeeper to have two separate closets - one where he let Lynne store her sexy nighties, and another where Jean kept her things. He had treated her to exotic trips - Warsaw, Rome, Paris - but never one to the altar.

Then came the sensational 'Scarsdale Letter', a classic piece of poison penmanship. It mentioned that Tarnower had changed his will against her - again,

School. But the relationship was slowly disintegrating as Jean became aware of her partner's more-than-passing interest in Lynne Tryforos, his medical assistant.

It was never disputed that Jean Harris killed Herman Tarnower - she admitted it herself. She drove, on 10 March 1980, five hours from her home in Virginia to Tarnower's Scarsdale mansion.

She entered the bedroom, saw negligées that were not hers, and then shot her lover

---

She planned to kill herself, she said, intending to see him one more time before pulling the trigger in front of his eyes. Armed with a Harrington and Richardson .32-calibre revolver, she arrived shortly before 10pm.

In his bedroom she saw negligées in the closet that did not belong to her.

She shot him.

She was standing outside in the pouring rain with a bunch of daisies in her hand when the police arrived an hour later to arrest her. Her lover, still alive, was gurgling incoherently in his death throes, four bullets in his head and body.

'What happened?' asked the cop.

'The doctor's been shot,' she replied.

'Where is he?'

a possible motive for murder. The letter, posted to Tarnower on the morning of the day that he died, was read to the court with electrifying effect:

I am distraught as I write this - your phone call to tell me that you preferred the company of a vicious, adulterous psychotic was topped by a call from the Dean of Students ten minutes later and has kept me awake for almost 36 hours...What I say will ramble but it will be the truth - and I have to do something besides shriek with pain...

Having just, not four weeks before, received a copy of your will with my name vigorously scratched out, and Lynne's name in your handwriting written in three places, leaving her a quarter of a million dollars and her children $25,000 apiece - and the boys and me nothing. It is the sort of thing I have almost grown accustomed to from Lynne... It isn't your style, but then Lynne has changed your

Below: *During her trial Jean Harris painted a vivid picture of years of emotional torture at the hands of cynical manipulator Tarnower. She was still sentenced to a minimum of fifteen years imprisonment.*

style. It is the culmination of 14 years of broken promises...

It didn't matter all that much, really - all I ever asked for was to be with you - and when I left you to know when we would see each other again so there would be something in life to look forward to. Now you are taking that away from me too and I am unable to cope...

To be jeered at, and called 'old and pathetic' made me seriously consider borrowing $5,000 and telling a doctor to make me young again - to do anything but not make me feel like discarded trash.

Medical testimony revealed that Jean Harris was on amphetamines for depression, and that she had been steadily increasing the dosages. And the greater part of the witnesses called to give evidence testified that her lover was cool, cynical, manipulating...almost a man who deserved to die.

THE VERDICT

The trial revealed a classic crime of passion - but jurors found it differently. Her lawyers persuaded her to plead to accidental manslaughter, saying that it was 'definite' she would be acquitted. On 28 February 1981 she was found guilty of murder, sentenced to a minimum of fifteen years imprisonment.

In 1981 a US court gave Harris a lengthy prison sentence for a classic *crime passionnel*

Many saw it - and still do - as a miscarriage of justice. She has suffered three heart attacks behind bars, and her family continue to press for a pardon. There has been a groundswell of support for her since the late 1980s as a result of a poignant book written by her of prison life and its crushing indignities.

Shana Alexander, who wrote a book about the affair, said: 'For me the bottom line...is that the question put to the jurors - what was Jean's intent that night? - is one that simply cannot be dealt with by the mechanisms of law. Because you cannot cut open a person's head and look inside.'

A ROYAL SCANDAL
Edward and Lillie

The prim morality of Victorian society tolerated the Prince of Wales's affairs when they were conducted discreetly. But it was scandalized when he made the beautiful Lillie Langtry his 'official' mistress and paraded openly in public with her

Right: *Top notch...His Royal Highness the Prince of Wales as a young man.*

Opposite: *Lillie Langtry... the prince's fatal attraction for the striking beauty began when he was introduced to her at a private supper in London in 1877.*

Below: *Lillie Le Breton (later Lillie Langtry) with her family in the Channel Isles in 1864. Lillie stands beside her father, the Dean of Jersey.*

H e became known as Edward the Caresser, a cheeky sobriquet for the monarch who cared little for public opinion and even less for those who tried to thwart his dalliances. Edward VII was the last of the 'golden age' of monarchs before World War I came along to smash the old order for ever.

The Edwardian era that he gave his name to is remembered in nostalgic terms as a time of shooting parties, lawn tennis and croquet, an age altogether more relaxed than the decades of Victorian moral steadfastness. No wonder, for Edward was a well-known debaucher, a man given to gluttony and high living and possessed of a voracious sexual appetite which he satisfied in the bedrooms of his friends' wives as well as the bordellos of Europe.

Edward satisfied his voracious sexual appetite in the bedrooms of his friends' wives as well as the bordellos of Europe

---

It was the novelist Henry James who first dubbed him Edward the Caresser and indeed Bertie, as his friends and the masses referred to him, prided himself on his vast sexual experience.

His mother Queen Victoria, and stern father Prince Albert, made his early life miserable. There were regular beatings and lectures on the correct way for a member of the royal family to behave, and many latter-day psychologists have sought to explain away his insatiable

appetite for sexual conquests as some sort of prolonged youthful rebellion.

But there was nothing youthful about the manner in which the Prince of Wales - his title before ascending the throne - set about enjoying his hedonistic lifestyle. He lived for life's pleasures - huge ten- and twelve-course meals, endless games of baccarat and days at the splendid racecourses of Europe, shooting parties, yachting, the theatre and, in between everything, his marathon bouts of sex.

He lost his virginity at the age of nineteen while serving with the British Army in Ireland. Some of his fellow officers smuggled an actress named Nellie Clifden into his bed at the Curragh camp. It was not to be the final whiff of scandal surrounding young Bertie.

His gambling and womanizing were to continue to land him in trouble. Twice Britain witnessed the scandal of his appearing in court - although as a witness, not as the accused.

Once was over a gambling feud, the second occasion when Lady Harriet Mordaunt insisted that her child, born blind, was a curse from God for her many adulterous relationships, including one with the Prince. He testified he was not the lady's lover, but speculation has remained rife to this day that he may have added perjury to his many other sins.

Below left: The cigar-smoking Edward, Prince of Wales in 1869. He had not yet met the woman who was to change his life - and scandalize society.

Below: When the prince met Lillie he leaned over to tell her that no pictures did justice to her beauty. Within a week they were lovers.

THE JERSEY LILY

In 1877, when he was thirty-six years old, his path crossed with that of a woman called Lillie Langtry and English society was never quite the same again. Although he - and many men of his aristocratic upbringing - indulged in mistresses, it was never the done thing to be seen to be parading them in public. They were kept for discreet dalliances and private dinners in clubs, well away from the glare of a disapproving, moralistic society.

What Edward did was to fly into the face of the English Establishment and flaunt his 'Jersey Lily' with abandon. For ten years his liaison with the showgirl scandalized Europe and the world, and it is said that in the House of Windsor to

Above: *A caricature of the Prince of Wales. He was a dandy who could not control his sexual adventures.*

Left: *King Edward VII... although married to Princess Alexandra of Denmark, he flaunted his 'Jersey Lily' to the world.*

this day there has never been total forgiveness for his wicked, wicked ways.

Although married to Princess Alexandra of Denmark - his father insisted upon the union after the disgrace over the Curragh incident - the Prince was so bored in his useless existence that he was led further and further astray.

Speculation has remained rife to this day that the Prince of Wales may have added perjury to his other sins

---

There were no stately duties for him - his mother had no intention of relinquishing the throne - and so his teeth sank into the pursuit of pleasure and never let go. His fatal attraction to Lillie Langtry began when he was introduced to her at a private supper thrown by his bachelor friend Sir Allen Young at his London home on 27 May 1877.

Lillie was a mysterious newcomer to the London social scene. Described as an actress, she had escaped from a stifling and puritanical existence which offered her no excitement and little hope. She was the only daughter of William Corbet le Breton, Dean of Jersey, in whose rectory she was born in 1853.

Perhaps it was her father's insatiable sexual appetite that made her the woman she was. Her father was known as the

'Dirty Dean' due to endless philandering. Indeed, he had to separate her from her first suitor when she was seventeen because the boy in question was one of his many illegitimate children!

Her only thought as she grew up was to escape her humdrum life and use her stunning looks to her own advantage - and stunning she was. She had a Grecian nose, flawless skin, large violet eyes, a perfect figure and hair that fell loosely in a cascade around her shoulders.

Lillie's clergyman father was known as the 'Dirty Dean' because of his endless capacity for womanizing

---

That alone was a shocking departure from the well-coiffed conventions of the period. One writer described her thus: 'She did not use whalebone corsets either. The result was a blend of classical goddess and earthy peasant girl, of the alabaster pedestal set amid the haystack.'

For Lillie, growing up with six brothers in the bucolic isolation of Jersey,

Top: *Bedchamber of a mistress. Lillie Langtry's boudoir around the year 1895.*

Above: *Fur-trimmed temptress Lillie Langtry so obsessed her royal escort that he turned her into his 'official' mistress.*

only her beauty seemed to offer a way out. She married Edward Langtry, the son of a prosperous Belfast shipowner who had come to live in Jersey with the sole intent of frittering away his father's money. He succumbed to her beauty and was whisked off to England as her hapless consort while she embarked on her quest for wealth and fame.

She had first come to the notice of London society two months before the supper party when, with her morose, dim-witted husband in tow, she had turned up at the home of a London socialite, Lady Sebright.

Whistler the artist was there, as were many prominent bright young things of the day. One of them, Frank Miles, saw the potential to turn Lillie into a 'PB' or professional beauty.

These were ladies of mostly genteel birth who were photographed in decent, though alluring, poses. Their portraits sold the length and breadth of Britain for the delectation of the lower classes. When Lillie was introduced to Bertie that first night - minus her husband - it was as the newest 'PB' on the circuit.

THE START OF THE AFFAIR

During supper with the prince he leaned over to tell her that she was even lovelier in the flesh than she was on cardboard. Ever the keen aficionado of beautiful women, he told her that he had seen several pictures of her, but that none did real justice to her 'radiant beauty'. Within a week they were lovers.

By the time of their first tryst Edward was already father to three children. To Edward, Victorian moral attitudes smacked of hypocrisy and, flawed though he most certainly was, hypocrisy was the one trait he was not prepared to condone.

He was a devoted and conscientious parent to his children, and tried as best he could to redeem his infidelities to his wife by being surprisingly frank with her about mistresses.

Princess Alexandra responded by treating his dalliances as though they were the childish pranks of some uncontrollable schoolboy.

Above: *Edward VII in dandified checked spats rests his foot on a 'wild' bull that he has shot at Chillingham Castle in Northumberland.*

The situation with Lillie Langtry, however, soon proved itself to be a relationship that went far beyond his usual flings with the well-bred ladies of Europe. For Edward soon began to insist that the relationship was recognized in society by turning her into his 'official' mistress. He escorted her to major public events such as Ascot races and built a love-nest for her at Bournemouth where, at one stage, he spent virtually every weekend. He even kissed her fully on the lips in public in Maxim's, the most famous restaurant in Paris.

For two years English society was agog at this spectacular new turn of events in the upper classes. Where there was no invitation to country house parties for Mrs Langtry, Edward simply wrote her name on the RSVP slip and brought her along. He even introduced her to his wife and to Queen Victoria in her drawing room at Buckingham Palace, because she was curious to see the creature who had exerted such an influence on her son.

Princess Alexandra responded to her husband's admissions of infidelity by treating them as schoolboy pranks

---

They travelled to Europe together, staying in the same suite at hotels in Paris and Monte Carlo. Cuckolded Ulsterman Edward Langtry could no longer take the humiliation and ran off to a future of debt and heavy drinking while his wife was paraded at the best restaurants as the most stunning woman of her age.

All went swimmingly for two years for the Prince and his showgirl - she still harboured ambitions to take to the stage - until she fell ill one night at his London home. Edward's wife summoned medical assistance, and she was packed off home while the doctor broke the news to Edward and his wife that she was pregnant.

Speculation and accusation have reverberated to this day that the child, a daughter born in secrecy in France and called Jeanne-Marie, was Bertie's baby.

But there was another rumour which has never been laid to rest - that Lillie, while indulging in the affair with Edward, had another lover, the young

Prince Louis of Battenberg. Royal gossip has it that for eighteen months both affairs ran in tandem, with Louis ever eager to share her bed when Bertie was elsewhere.

Whatever the truth, Lillie hid the identity of her daughter from the world and passed her off as her niece, telling the child that her natural father, Lillie's brother, had died while in India.

FROM BOUDOIR TO STAGE

Public interest in Lillie seemed to wane in the two years after the child's birth. By some bizarre social convention of the time she seemed to have angered those 'Professional Beauty' admirers by having a young child, and found herself frozen out on the edges of the circle she once thought herself to be an important part of.

The Prince continued to offer her his patronage and his boudoir, but even he was forced to distance himself from her somewhat. It is said that he actively encouraged and helped her to achieve the career she had always fancied for herself - the stage. She made her professional debut at the Haymarket Theatre on 15 December 1881 playing the role of Kate Hardcastle in *She Stoops to Conquer*.

The Prince of Wales, his wife and many figures from London society were there to see her performance and ensured enthusiastic applause and encores - a level of enthusiasm which was not, however, shared by the critics. Eva, one of the pre-eminent theatrical reviewers of the day, said caustically: 'She has small ability, no more than that of the respectable amateur,' while the satirical magazine *Punch* scalded her with: 'As a novice she should first master the art of acting.' Perhaps the *Times* best summed up the feelings of the day when it commented: 'At least the audience got their money's worth.'

The town of Vinegaroo, Texas, was so captivated by her that the local council voted to change its name to Langtry

---

Despite the critics' coolness the 'Jersey Lily', as she was soon dubbed, continued to bloom in her new career. Americans, enchanted by the royal scandal, flocked to England and became her greatest fans as her touring company took theatres all over Britain by storm.

Within the space of five years she became known as the toughest and most prestigious actress of her time. She visited New York in 1882 to rapturous applause and her wealth increased spectacularly. On the same visit she went to the Texas town of Vinegaroo, which was so taken by her that the town council voted to change its name permanently to Langtry.

European, American and domestic touring did little for the royal relationship, but Bertie seemed content to let his mistress have her head. He was as much impressed with material gain as he was with beautiful women, and when both were

Below: *Resplendent in his state robes, the King of England looked the picture of Establishment respectability.*

As with all his affairs the relationship began to wither, but she remained on close terms with him for the remainder of his life. He went on to bed a succession of new conquests - among them the French theatrical star Sarah Bernhardt, the 'Madonna' of her day - and she found solace in the arms of many wealthy society men. The Prime Minister, Gladstone, was rumoured to be among them.

In 1897 she married Hugo De Bathe, whom she had met two years previously. In 1907 her husband became a baronet and Lillie became Lady de Bathe.

The Jersey Lily lived until 1929. She had seen the 'golden age' and its manhood destroyed in the foulest war man had ever waged, and was heart-broken by the slaughter on the western front. She went into a decline after the war, claiming her heart was shattered at the loss of so many fine young men, and was buried in the same tiny churchyard as her father back on the island where she was born.

Her husband, the poor, cuckolded Ulsterman who had brought his magnetic wife to London, had died several years before in Chester lunatic asylum. He had been found wandering about Crewe railway station, dazed and with a serious cut to his head. He was carted away and incarcerated for claiming to be married to the great Lillie Langtry!

combined he found the mix irresistible.

In 1975 royal letters were unearthed that showed the depth of his feeling for her and how he always seemed to be prepared to put her career ahead of the romance they shared. On 5 September 1885, while on a visit to the Swedish royal family in Stockholm, he wrote, 'I am glad to hear you are in harness again and most sincerely wish you all the possible success in your tour though I fear you have very hard work before you. I am glad to have the list of towns in which you are to play. Since the 2nd I am the King's guest in Sweden. I told him I had heard from you and he particularly begged to be remembered to you and wish you success in your profession.'

In another letter he wrote of the sadness he felt at her leaving for a long American tour, but finished the note off with the words: 'Perhaps you are right to make hay while the sun shines.' Another, addressed to 'Ma Chère Amie', said: 'You are so busy...and so am I!'

*Above: **Still striking in later life...Lillie Langtry as Lady de Bathe in 1928.***

*Right: **Lillie takes a stroll in Hyde Park in 1911. As Edward's passion began to fade, she took on new lovers - including the great Liberal statesman Gladstone, according to one distinctly unlikely rumour.***

UNITY MITFORD
Hitler's English Rose

As the shadow of war loomed in the 1930s an upper-class English rose flirted with Nazism and became an Adolf Hitler 'groupie'. Her obsession ended in tragedy in a Munich park

Life at the crazy court of Adolf Hitler veered between the normal and the insane, from the spartan to the luxurious, and the people that the Fuehrer collected around him reflected the madness of those days like bevelled mirrors.

As well as the usual fawning circus of Nazi flunkeys, in the 1930s a woman entered the inner circle who had the same kind of mesmeric effect on him that he had upon others. Unity Valkyrie Freeman-Mitford was the spellbinder who earned the scorn of her own countrymen when she became a member of the elite clique who had Hitler's ear.

Nothing could have seemed a more absurd proposition. He was the working-class, embittered Austrian corporal who had seized power on a mandate of abolishing the old order in favour of his hypnotic National Socialism. She was to the manner born, a lady of high breeding, the daughter of a dazzling family of aristocrats who belonged to another age.

Together they formed what the French have long termed a *folie à deux* - the madness between two people. Electricity crackled between them as Unity preached to England that Hitler was the Messiah to be obeyed, not fought.

'I want everyone to know I am a Jew-hater,' she wrote to the Nazi paper *Der Sturmer*. 'England for the English! Out with the Jews! *Heil Hitler*!'

In a short time she had become an ever-increasing influence on the monster destined to lead the world into the most destructive war in history. And yet, seemingly as quickly as the spell was woven, it was broken. Hitler's invasion of Poland in 1939 plunged Unity back into an appalling reality - one that had been clouded, as it had been clouded for millions of decent Germans, by the image of the swastika.

Unity shot herself days after the war began and never recovered from the wounds, although it would take her another eight agonizing years to die. Her journey from gifted English rose to maniacal Fascist and back again was one of the the strangest stories to come from those turbulent times.

A FAMILY OF ECCENTRICS

It all began in August 1914, the start of World War I. But Unity's family was a throwback, a time-warped hybrid of Victorian and Edwardian morals and values that her father, Lord Redesdale, intended to preserve. He brought up Unity, her five sisters and one brother to respect the 'old order', even as it was dying in the shellholes and trenches of the Western Front.

The Mitford girls were a remarkable family. Diana went on to marry Sir Oswald Mosley, who founded the British Union of Fascists. Nancy became a writer – penning among other books *The*

Above: *Unity Valkyrie Freeman-Mitford made no bones about her anti-Semetic views.*

Opposite: *Three sisters at a friend's wedding in 1932... Unity Mitford (left) with Diana and Nancy.*

Below: *One of a literary family, Jessica Mitford shows her autobiography to husband Bob Treuhaft.*

Pursuit of Love – as did Jessica. Unity achieved infamy over fame, but none the less made her mark on the world.

She was brought up mostly at home at Swinbrook in Oxfordshire, where a series of governesses and her mother taught her privately. As a teenager she did the 'regular debutante thing', as she herself put it, and acquired a reputation as a partygoer and prankster. One of her favourite tricks was pulling out her pet rat 'Ratular' from her handbag at posh country house balls to stroke him in front of her horrified hosts!

Unity was addicted to practical jokes and would take her pet rat in her handbag to smart balls

---

Hers was a world without want or cares. As the industrialized nations of the world slumped into history's greatest depression, Unity could well have frittered away her life as a 'bright young thing'. Instead, in 1932 she changed direction when she was hypnotized by the rise of Fascism.

Sir Oswald Mosley, with his legions of blackshirts, was the British attempt at Fascism, the fervent movement that had rooted itself in Germany and Italy and would soon flourish in Spain. For many, torn between the Communists of the Soviet Union and the crumbling *anciens regimes* of the West, Fascism seemed a viable, vibrant, promising new creed.

THE LURE OF THE BLACKSHIRTS

With her sister Diana, Unity thrust herself wholeheartedly into the party. In August 1933, as a member of the delegation of the British Union of Fascists, she attended the light-and-sound spectacular of the first Nuremberg Rally since Hitler had seized power.

Watching the searchlights arcing through the misty air, the blazing hand-held torches, the solid blocks of men marching to guttural songs, Unity's dreams were fuelled as never before.

Below: *Adolf Hitler and his mistress Eva Braun with their dogs at Berchtesgaden. Unity Mitford was a favoured visitor.*

Mein Kampf - Hitler's new testament - she arrived at the school in Munich. Run by Baroness Laroche, the school was intended as an establishment 'to nourish the body and soul of young females in preparation for the life which awaits them outside these portals'. But Unity was not interested in any lessons or marquetry classes. 'It was her chance to lay siege to Hitler,' said biographer David Pryce-Jones, who penned an authoritative work on her.

It was with the persistence of the dizziest fan after a beloved pop star. Perhaps she should be regarded as the prototype groupie.

The Mitfords were in my opinion terribly sinister. I do believe it's people like that who sign the death warrant. They would say to their friends: 'Of course we'll shoot you, but you can have a darling little cigarette first.' They were part of that upper-class English group - from the Duke of Windsor down - who had the makings of an embryonic Fascist state...Our bacon was saved from them at the eleventh hour!

Once Unity was in Munich, she soon learned Hitler's favourite spots in the city. She calculated where the best places would be to effect an introduction to the great man and decided in the end on the Osteria Bavaria restaurant. No one ever had any idea when Hitler would drop in unannounced at the restaurant to eat

She drank it all in and believed in the gospel of hate the Nazis were preaching.

Photographs of her at the time showed her with William Joyce, better known to a generation of English people as Lord Haw-Haw, the sycophantic Nazi lover who was later to die on Allied gallows for treason. She was also pictured with various Nazi bigwigs.

But only one man, holding hypnotic sway over the massed ranks before him, interested her. 'The first moment I saw Adolf Hitler, I knew there was no one else I would rather meet,' she said.

If England had been defeated in 1940, Unity would probably have been Hitler's PR in an office in Downing Street

---

Above: *Street rabble rouser. Sir Oswald Mosley gives a fascist salute as he leads a march through London at the end of 1937.*

Below: *Lord and Lady Redesdale with daughter Unity and her German Embassy escort Dr Fitz-Randolph at an Anglo-German Fellowship concert at Christmas 1938.*

Back in England, she became a celebrity. Hitler, with his toothbrush moustache and lopsided haircut, was still something of a joke, and the thought of a young woman as well connected as Unity Mitford being entranced by him was a source of endless gossip. One cartoon in the *News Chronicle* newspaper showed Unity hiding behind a strident Hitler with the caption: 'You can't criticize Unity with impunity. If you try to belittle 'er, you have to answer to Hitler!'

She was nineteen on her return, and imbued now with the full passion of National Socialism. She persuaded her doting father to send her to a German finishing school - the perfect place to arrange a meeting with the Fuehrer.

Armed with an English translation of

German noodles and drink - contrary to popular myth that he was completely teetotal - a little Rhine wine or beer mixed with water.

THE FATEFUL MEETING

Saturday, 9 February 1935, seems to be the date that destiny smiled on Unity. Relaxing there with party functionaries, Hitler saw the petite blonde and sent over a flunkey with an invitation that she should join him for lunch. Her friend, a woman known only as Mary, recorded in her diary: 'Hitler sent for Unity on Saturday and she had lunch at his table. Thrilled to death, of course!'

Unity had made it known to her and her other friends at the school that the boys who wooed them at tea dances held no interest for her. Politically - and, some would later suggest sexually - she only had eyes for Adolf Hitler.

Lienritte von Schirach, daughter of Nazi photographer Heinrich Hoffman, recalled how Hitler became increasingly fascinated with 'the English Lord's daughter'. She witnessed the way Unity wove herself, with her faltering German, into his inner circle, against the advice of people like Rudolf Hess, Hitler's deputy, who feared she might be a British spy.

Frau von Schirach said: *Hitler was caught up not only in her beauty, but also her social position... Hitler fell under her spell and refused to believe those who*

Above: *Fanatical about her politics, obsessive about her men... Unity had eyes only for Adolf Hitler.*

Below: *Unity Mitford arrives on a stretcher at Folkestone on her ignominious return to Britain.*

said she could be a spy. He preferred to trust his own instinctive understanding of people. He also used her to relay his ideas to Britain.

Unity moved out of the school and into a room at a Munich University students' hostel. She bought copies of *Der Sturmer*, which portrayed Jews as pigs and rats, and bedecked her dressing table with pictures of the Nazi hierarchy. She also immersed herself in the writings of Alfred Rosenberg, the Nazis' quack racial theorist.

The pin-ups on Unity's dressing table were not film stars but senior members of the Nazi party

---

On 26 May 1935 the British public learned just how brightly the torch she was carrying for Adolf Hitler burned. A *Sunday Express* correspondent interviewed her about her life in Germany. Sefton Delmer wrote: *Her eyes lit with enthusiasm as she spoke to me of Hitler. 'The hours I have spent in his company,' she said, 'are some of the most impressive in my life. The entire German nation is lucky to have such a great personality as its head.' As I left her in the students' home in which she has lived for the last year, she raised her arm in the Nazi salute and cried: 'Heil Hitler!'*

DESPISED IN EUROPE AND ENGLAND

By many Unity was seen as a naive young woman seeking to absolve her class guilt by riding on the coat-tails of Nazism. They claimed that she could not possibly know anything about the Nuremberg decrees which stripped Jews of their rights as citizens, nor of the camp at Dachau where political opponents were incarcerated and murdered.

But what, in many eyes, made Unity fascinated with Nazism is that she *did* know what was going on. She became a familiar face in Hitler's entourage, and in the summer of 1936 she addressed a huge crowd gathered on the Hesselberg Mountain near Nuremberg. There she espoused the full venom of the Nazis' twisted philosophy, saying that she thought Dachau was the best place for the

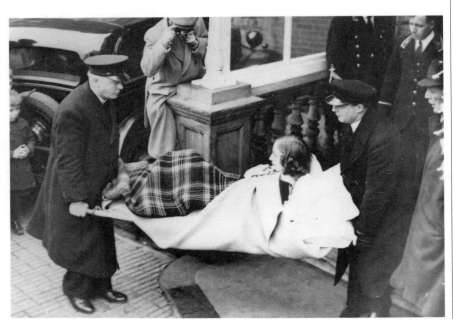

Jews and that only under Hitler could the 'lesser races' of the East be subdued.

In England there was no longer curiosity about Unity but derision and hatred. She had nailed her colours firmly to those of the crooked cross as Europe braced itself for the coming conflict.

At Fascist rallies in England Unity needed police protection to save her from the wrath of the crowds

---

Unity even had to be rescued by police when she returned to England to attend a Hyde Park Fascist rally, and the crowd of demonstrators opposed to them tried to hurl her into the Serpentine.

Unity was not without patriotism for her own country. She deeply loved England and justified her pro-Hitler sentiment by claiming it was the only political system that could save a fragmented Europe. 'I followed with despair the political developments surrounding relations between Britain and Germany,' cried Unity, torn between the love of two flags and two utterly different philosophies.

HITLER'S PROTEGEE

She returned to Germany. In 1936 Hitler took her to Bayreuth, one of the premier opera festivals of Europe and one that he had commandeered and turned into a showcase exhibition of German 'art'.

But after his rise to power art had very little to do with it, and the festival became instead a celebration of stirring Wagnerian music which embodied his concept of Germanic greatness.

Albert Speer, the one member of the inner circle who could be said to be a true intellectual, was convinced she was besotted with him, while he was spellbound by her. 'She was highly in love with him,' he declared. *It was hero worship of the highest order. I doubted if he ever did more than take her hand in his... She was the only woman -whose opinions he listened to... In discussions over tea...she would always be willing to argue a point, to try to make him see something another way, and he would be tolerant and always willing to listen.*

Hitler had moved her into a gracious pension in Munich, and began sending an SS staff car over each afternoon to collect and deliver her to his own apartment for afternoon tea and the gooey cream cakes he relished so much.

She was even a privileged visitor to the Eagle's Nest, his mountain retreat high above Berchtesgaden, where he would hold long conversations with her. He used her as the divining rod for understanding British political thought and wanted Britain to use its Navy to patrol its imperial outposts - not to turn it against German shipping.

What Unity told Hitler at these cosy chats can only be guessed at. But by this time she had become such a committed Nazi, it can only be conjectured that she agreed with him and spurred him on.

Experts believe, however, that while she may have found herself falling in love with him, Hitler never wavered from his mistress Eva Braun, and it is thought

Below: *Unity is helped by her parents on her return to England, sick and in disgrace after her dalliance with the Nazis.*

Above: Hitler acknowledges the adulation of the masses as he takes the salute on his fiftieth birthday with Mussolini and Goering.

secretary to Hitler, was personally ordered by his master to arrange a selection for her to choose from. She eventually picked one with magnificent rococo ceilings and french windows that led on to a terrace.

THE FINAL TERRIBLE DECISION

Unity returned to England to collect English antiques to furnish her new apartment. But while she criss-crossed the Channel, Adolf Hitler was drawing up plans for the annihilation of Poland.

Unity had no idea that war was just around the corner. Up until then she had seen Hitler's moves against other sovereign states - Austria, Czecho-slovakia - as territorial rights. She could soothe her conscience with the balm of 'rightful possession', but an aggressive war which threatened the peace of the world was another matter.

Most people agree it is unlikely that the Fuehrer's relationship with his English admirer was ever a sexual one

---

Two days before the invasion of Poland on 1 September she pleaded with the British ambassador in Berlin to give an assurance that Britain would not be dragged into war. When no such assurance was forthcoming Unity was plunged into depression. She was now truly torn between two nations that she cared deeply for: she had to choose.

Two days later, when England found itself at war, Unity could take no more. She went to the Gauleiter of Munich, Adolf Wagner, and pushed into his hands a brown envelope. Wagner recalled: 'She wept, she could not speak. In the envelope was her Nazi party badge, a picture of Hitler and a letter to the Fuehrer in which she said she could no longer find a reason to live.'

In a grand, romantic-tragic gesture, she took a small calibre handgun with her to the English Garden, in the centre of Munich, put it to her temple and pulled the trigger. The bullet lodged in her brain - far enough in to be beyond the reach of surgeons, but not far enough to kill her.

She was found by park officials and

that the two women never met. Like Speer, biographers of Unity believe her infatuation never blossomed into a sexual relationship. Eva was intensely jealous of the prim Englishwoman, and once referred to her in a temper as 'that damned English Valkyrie'!

Every day Hitler sent a car to Unity's Munich apartment to collect her for afternoon tea

---

In the summer of 1939 Europe basked in a heatwave. Unity was back in Munich and had now been given an exquisite apartment in the Agnesstrasse, a fashionable address in the heart of the city. Martin Bormann, sinister personal

rushed to the university clinic where the best surgeons in Germany, on the orders of Hitler, endeavoured to save her. The Fuehrer was at her side within twenty-four hours. Aides said they had never seen their leader as shaken before.

He used German intelligence contacts in Switzerland to get a message through to her parents in England to tell them what had happened.

Hitler gaver orders to Germany's finest surgeons to save her life

---

There were tears in his eyes on the night of 8 November 1939, when he saw Unity for the last time in the hospital. She asked him then if she could be sent back to England. He agreed that it was the best course of events, but advised her to wait a little longer until she was stronger.

THE JOURNEY HOME

By the spring of 1940, shortly before he was to unleash his panzer blitzkrieg on France and the Low Countries, he ordered a first class railway carriage to be converted into a travelling hospital ward. One of his personal physicians accompanied Unity to Zurich, where an English doctor awaited her arrival. The journey continued through the south of France to one of the Channel ports, where Lord Redesdale waited to take his daughter back into the country that despised her.

'So ended the story of the remarkable relationship between a woman and Hitler,' said Frau von Schirach.

Above: *Released from detention at the end of the war, Sir Oswald and Lady Mosley hid at the Shaven Crown Inn, Oxfordshire.*

Below: *Sir Oswald Mosley whipping up support at the formation conference of his new Union Movement in the spring of 1948.*

A woman who, like few others in Hitler's circle, showed independence and enterprise. She had not fallen prey to the Fuehrer, like so many other women. As an Englishwoman of the aristocracy she was never subject to the rule that woman must be man's devoted servant; but she had fallen prey to his ideas and her own, so that she failed to notice for far too long where this man and his policies were actually leading.

Unity arrived at Folkestone amid a national furore, with an armed guard meeting her; there was a clamour for her internment. But she escaped detention and retreated to the family's Scottish island, Inchkenneth, for recuperation.

She lived in a kind of twilight zone throughout the war, finally succumbing to her injurites in 1948. Hitler continued to care deeply for her and for two years afterwards could not talk of the suicide attempt. When Munich came under Allied air assault later in the war he issued a decree to save her belongings.

Since her death her life has been studied in minute detail, many apologists for her pointing out that in the end the spell woven by Hitler was finally and irrevocably broken. But one story persists. It was after the Coventry firebombing, one of the worst during the blitz against Britain, which destroyed the cathedral and cost hundreds of lives. The story goes that Unity sat up in bed and said: 'Such a tragedy ... we lost twenty of our best bombers.'

Hardly the remark of a penitent.

KISS AND TELL
Dangerous Liaisons

The lure of a younger woman has broken many a marriage and destroyed many a career. Sometimes men even marry them - with equally dire consequences. When such scandal attaches to public figures there is no privacy and no mercy

Question: What do Bible-thumping evangelist Jimmy Swaggart, mega-tycoon Donald Trump and former aspiring US President Gary Hart have in common? Answer: They're all victims of bimbo-itis - that dread malady which has toppled titans and pummelled politicians almost since time began.

The malady has affected bishops, boxers and billionaires, and turned otherwise 'normal' men into love-sick sycophants who sometimes risked - and lost - all to carry on their relationships with younger women.

Hart lost his chance to become President. Actor Rob Lowe may have lost his career, and certainly his reputation. Donald Trump lost some $25 million thanks to his affair with Georgia peach Marla Maples. And TV preacher Jim Bakker lost his freedom.

Women it seems, still have the power to make or break their men.

THE GREASY POLE OF POLITICS

Unlike some of her 'peers', Donna Rice has eschewed the spotlight - save for one promotional stint for a jeans company - since her 1987 affair with Senator Hart ruined his chance to make the Oval Office. The leggy, blonde model is virtually in hiding these days, studying acting and performing with a small community theatre in northern Virginia.

'She wants to remain private,' said Tricia Erickson, who provided 'crisis management' when Rice hit the headlines. 'She's been doing volunteer work, helping the disabled and the terminally ill. She could have exploited her own situation - I had a couple of million dollars' worth of offers on my desk - but she chose to have her self-respect and dignity.'

And unlike some, Donna isn't making a mint out of her brief encounter with infamy. In fact, she's been living with a

Opposite: *Donald Trump, said to have lost $25 million due to his love affair with 'Georgia peach' Marla Maples.*

Left: *Ivana Trump, who took her tycoon husband to the cleaners over his highly publicised affair with Marla.*

Below: *Openly unfaithful... Trump squired mistress Marla Maples to many showbusiness events during their dalliance.*

ceremony with Hart in which they 'brushed the front and back of our bodies with eagle feathers...it was sensual'.

Incredibly, once his reputation as a womanizer started to haunt his presidential campaign, Hart took the extraordinary step of daring the media to follow him in a bid to clear his name and show he was a hard-working politician.

'It was sensual,' confirmed the Comanche lady of a ceremony at which she and Senator Hart brushed each other's bodies with eagle's feathers

---

One newspaper, the *Miami Herald*, took him up on the offer, and their story about his weekend tryst with Rice rocked America. It became apparent that Hart and the leggy blonde had been 'friends' for four months, and had even been on an overnight sailing trip to the Caribbean aboard the aptly named *Monkey Business*.

Despite Hart's repeated denials of any impropriety, including the public show of support from his loyal wife, he saw his popularity go into a tailspin.

family in the Washington area and helps with the chores for pocket money.

Hart has largely retired to private life since his tryst with Rice. But the bubbly blonde wasn't the first woman the one-time senator knew intimately. Indeed, he admitted he had cheated on his wife, Lee, during two separations in 1979 and 1981.

The first liaison was with Diana Phillips, described as a professional hostess. The other was with Lynn Carter, prominent in Iowa politics. But during his presidential campaign one magazine also linked him to a 'radiant divorcee', whom he described as his 'spiritual adviser'.

Marilyn Youngbird, an American Indian, said she took part in a Comanche

Above: *Donna Rice hit the headlines and ruined Democratic presidential candidate Gary Hart's political career.*

Right: *Senator Gary Hart and his wife campaigning for the Democratic nomination. His smile turned to a scowl when he read of his affair with Donna Rice.*

STARS OF SCREEN AND BEDROOM

Jan Parsons will never be a household name like Rice, but her sizzling one-night stand with actor Rob Lowe during the Democratic Convention in Atlanta in 1989 has been captured for ever on videotape.

Jan, who was just sweet sixteen when she, Lowe and another girlfriend engaged in a steamy *menage à trois*, dropped from sight soon after the scandal erupted. Lowe was later 'punished' for his misdeed with twenty hours of community service.

Jan used to work at the Super Hair Three-13 beauty salon, but her current whereabouts remain a mystery. She was a regular on the Atlanta nightclub scene when she met Lowe at the Club Rio, and was reportedly part of a group which engaged in kinky sex and devil worship.

In fact, in divorce proceedings between her parents, her mother, Lena Ann Wilson, claimed that Jan's father 'engaged in strange rituals in a hidden space in the closet'.

Although Lowe has made a couple of films since the scandal unfolded, his career has stalled.

Lowe's problems weren't the first time a Hollywood hero had fallen victim to a *femme fatale*. In fact Hollywood's greatest rogue, the dashing star Errol Flynn, saw his career sink to the bottom. Two sordid rape cases helped to shatter his screen persona and pushed him into a world of drugs and alcohol.

'I was attacked as a sex criminal,' he said after his 1943 trial for statutory rape. 'I knew I could never escape this brand, that I would always be associated in the public mind with an internationally followed rape case.'

He was right - even though he won the case, the Australian-born hell-raiser went into a decline. He was thirty-three when seventeen-year-old Betty Hansen and sixteen-year-old Peggy La Rue Satterlee cried rape to the Hollywood police.

Flynn's 'sexcapades' began early, and he was just seventeen when he left school - in a hurry. 'I was caught with the daughter of a laundress,' he recalled in his best-selling book, *My Wicked, Wicked Ways*.

When he was 'discovered' and brought to Hollywood, he was like the kid in the proverbial candy store, and fast became a

Top: *Movie actress Julia Roberts ditched her husband-to-be Kiefer Sutherland after his publicized party romps with a nightclub dancer.*

Above: *Kiefer Sutherland won and then lost the love of* **Pretty Woman** *star Julia Roberts because of his hell-raising.*

sought-after stud with his rugged good looks and colonial charm. He called himself 'a walking phallic symbol'.

'He was changing women as fast as his valet could change the sheets,' said Nora Eddington, the actor's second wife.

Seeing his accuser's hairy legs Errol Flynn knew that, drunk or sober, he could never have contemplated sex with her

---

He raged his way through Tinsel Town - fights, booze and women, always women. Even his yacht was named *Cirrhosis-by-the-Sea*, and his mansion on Mulholland Drive came complete with an orgy room and two-way mirrored ceiling. Flynn would later write that, as soon as he saw his accuser's hairy legs, 'I knew I was innocent. Drunk, sober, drugged, partly insane, these were not the legs Flynn would have next to his.' He died in 1959 at the age of forty-nine - his great energy and lust for life had been burned out.

And just recently, Hollywood actor Kiefer Sutherland saw his hopes of marrying *Pretty Woman* Julia Roberts go up in smoke, partly because of his relationship with a nightclub dancer called Amanda Rice.

Sutherland and Roberts were all set to be married in the splashiest wedding Tinsel Town had seen in years. The expected cost was put at $1 million.

According to his nightclub dancer friend, Kiefer Sutherland likened Julia Roberts to a corpse in bed

---

But just three days before the wedding Julia got cold feet because of her fears of failing at marriage, like her parents, and Sutherland's continued trysts with other women, particular Rice.

Amanda, a stripper, even blabbed to the media that Sutherland had told her that 'making love to Julia was like having sex with a corpse'.

HEAVYWEIGHT HUMILIATION

Mike Tyson was equally damaged by his brief, stormy marriage to Robin Givens (although she, too, suffered at the hands of the ex-champ). She publicly humiliated him by calling him a total basket case on national television and describing life with him as 'pure hell'. It's a reputation confirmed during Tyson's trial for the rape of an eighteen-year-old beauty queen in 1992, and Robin, who's still busy with her acting career, hasn't changed her opinion since the 1989 divorce.

'Mike should be required to wear a sign that says, "Caution: Mike Tyson is hazardous to women," ' she said. 'He's a demon underneath. He's got a terrible temper. I was terrified of him.' And, she claims, he put her mother, Ruth Roper, into hospital. 'He literally broke her heart,' she said.

Still, there are many who believe Givens contrived to marry the former

Opposite: *Robin Givens humiliated husband Mike Tyson by calling him a 'basket case' on American television.*

Below: *Mike Tyson surrenders to the authorities after being indicted on rape charges in Indianapolis in 1991. In February 1992 he was found guilty of raping a 'Miss Black America' beauty contestant.*

champ for his wealth, and was banking on divorcing him from the beginning. Her apparent rush to establish residence in California - which has strict communal property laws - did nothing to dispel these notions.

THE 'QUEEN OF MEAN'

Hotel magnate Harry Helmsley has had his reputation dragged through the mud by his own wife. While Leona Helmsley may not fit the physical mould of the average bimbo - she's not exactly young or beautiful - she has cost her husband untold damage because of her greed.

The 'Queen of Mean' made Harry a laughing stock. She unwittingly depicted him as a befuddled, senile fool who could

no longer run his empire.

Some long-time associates of seventy-nine-year-old Helmsley say the tycoon was a decent chap before his marriage to Leona in 1972. But afterwards Harry, a reclusive type, underwent a dramatic change, hitting the party circuit.

Actor Cliff Robertson remembers one of the parties that Leona threw. 'Leona ...showed us her pool, had photographers there as soon as you walked in,' he recalled. 'I just thought it was a rather ostentatious display of new wealth. I thought it was, in a way, rather sad. I felt sorry for Harry. He seemed very nice. I couldn't wait to get home, frankly.'

Leona, who was sentenced on multiple tax charges in 1990, moved a step closer to a four-year jail sentence in July 1991 when an appeals court rejected her plea to overturn the conviction.

Leona Helmsley's court battles have cost her husband Harry an estimated $20 million

---

However, the federal court left one small glimmer of hope for the seventy-one-year-old tyrant, by finding technical flaws in four of the thirty-three counts on which she was convicted. Still, federal prosecutors feel the ruling may only reduce her total fines and have no effect at all on her sentence.

So far, Leona's court battles have cost her and Harry an estimated $20 million.

But that's nothing compared to what Jessica Hahn cost Jim Bakker, the diminutive former television preacher.

HELLFIRE AND DAMNATION

Bakker was brought down by the former church secretary, whom he allegedly drugged and had sex with in a Florida hotel room a short prayer or two before he returned to the pulpit to admonish his flock for not following God's ways. The ensuing scandal eventually triggered a government probe into the good minister's fund-raising gimmicks, and resulted in a hefty prison term.

Hahn, meanwhile, has got on with her life. Following a few nip-and-tuck operations paid for by Hugh Hefner, she

Top and above: *Roxanne Pulitzer and her husband Peter faced each other across a Florida courtroom while scandalous allegations were made of their millionaire lifestyle.*

Murphree, now thirty, a prostitute with a record in two states, was the woman whom Swaggart regularly paid to perform sex acts while he watched in a seedy New Orleans hotel - and she kindly re-created the poses for *Penthouse*. She even went on a national media tour to promote her story of their sexual liaison.

Murphree said the evangelist, who scoffed at Bakker's problems until he, too, was caught, patronized her for more than a year. She went along with his requests while he paid the going rate, but became enraged when he suggested that her nine-year-old daughter watch them.

Swaggart eventually went on national television and tearfully confessed he had committed an unspecified 'moral sin' and stepped down from the pulpit.

A few months later the Assemblies of God defrocked Swaggart for rejecting a Church order to suspend his preaching for a year, which he said would destroy his $140 million a year worldwide ministries. When he returned to the pulpit, Swaggart told his congregation that the Lord had forgiven him for his sins and 'what's past is past'.

DOWN ON THE STUD FARM

Even the famed House of Gucci has not been spared. Fashion mogul Paolo Gucci and his opera-loving wife split up in 1991 amid charges of illicit barn-yard sex and big-bucks spending sprees.

The very visible split erupted when Jenny Gucci claimed that the fifty-nine-year-old Paolo had moved a stable girl less than half his age into the fourteenth-century English country house they had shared since their marriage fourteen years earlier. And she has vowed to make him pay for his dalliance.

Jilted Jenny says the other woman is pretty twenty-one-year-old Penny Armstrong, who works for Gucci on his stud farm. 'I mean, what do they talk about - heavy metal rock groups? A thirty-eight-year age difference is pretty enormous.'

The fashion king calls the allegations preposterous. 'Jenny has become a shrewd, materialistic wife. Any feelings I had for her are gone now...'

Ironically, the Manhattan judge presiding over the battle is the same one

posed nude in *Playboy* magazine, obtained work as a morning dee-jay in Phoenix, Arizona and has now launched her own telephone talk line. For the price of $2 anyone can call and get a recording of Jessica's hints for a better life.

'I wanted to be a saint and ended up a centrefold,' says the former church secretary who destroyed TV evangelist Jim Bakker

---

But the phone line also allows people to get to know the real Jessica. 'I want people to know that I'm not selfish. That I want to be useful,' she explained. 'I want to be used by God. I wanted to be a saint and ended up being a centrefold.'

Debra Murphree, the prostitute in the sex scandal that disgraced TV evangelist Jimmy Swaggart, never wanted to be a saint, but she too ended up a centrefold - in the rival *Penthouse* magazine.

who handled the drawn-out Trump split, which ended in Donald forking out almost $25 million.

At stake in the Gucci affair is Paolo's $50 million fortune. And both he and Jenny have vowed to fight to the finish.

'My wife has made a big mistake,' Gucci said. 'She is acting like Saddam Hussein. If she hadn't started a war, she would have got what she wanted. I have never denied her anything. But this is the way she paid me back - and now she is in danger of losing everything.'

Jenny, a tall English-born blonde who met the designer while studying opera in Italy, isn't deterred. 'I'm not acting like Hussein, he is. I'm Norman Schwarzkopf - and we all know who won.'

THE LOVE MATCH

In an unusual twist to the old story, tennis queen Martina Navratilova has also seen her name dragged through the mud by her lover, Texas socialite Judy Nelson.

Nelson has slapped a $10 million lawsuit on Martina and, in an historic move, filed a five-minute video recording along with the lawsuit.

Nelson, who gave up her husband to become Navratilova's lover in the 1980s,

Below: *Tennis ace Martina Navratilova and long-term lover Judy Nelson suffered emotional traumas as their affair ended in courtroom battles over money.*

says she and Martina were more than just bed partners. Her lawyer, Jerry Loftin, said: 'Judy is very saddened by the situation but there is no hope of a reconciliation. The contract was drawn up and filmed, and provides for an equal share of assets.'

Nelson is convinced she will win because she has film of herself and Navratilova signing their business contract

---

Nelson, who was dumped by Martina in 1991 for a younger woman, Cindy Nelson (no relation), also claims to have a tape of an interview in which Martina said that Judy was her partner 'in everything'.

Although Judy and Martina claim they were not 'married' at the time the contract was signed, some tennis insiders have confided that the couple did go through their own marriage ceremony, and actually exchanged rings.

Martina says Nelson's bitter lawsuit has put a shadow over what was supposed to be a satisfying conclusion to her magical career, which includes nine Wimbledon titles.

THE KENNEDYS
America's First Family

America's pride or America's shame? The Kennedy dynasty, the golden 'First Family', was involved with bootlegging, sexual debauchery, drugs and the Mafia - a web of vice and scandal that ultimately destroyed them as a political force

The Kennedy clan have been described as America's 'royal family'. For a country that has never enjoyed (or suffered from) a monarchy, the USA seems to have a strange yearning for the institution.

But if it is an oddity that such adulation exists at all, it is an even more imponderable enigma that, of all the candidates for such honours, it should be the Kennedys who emerged as the leading society lights. Because the family's background hardly lent itself to the elite role it came to follow...

The multi-million-dollar Kennedy dynasty was built on crime. Joseph Kennedy Sr, the colourful founder of the clan, was widely believed to have been a Prohibition-beating bootlegger in the twenties. Joe's grandfather made whiskey barrels and his father was a saloon keeper, so entering the drink trade himself was a natural step.

Nothing illegal was ever admitted or proved. How the Kennedys made their early fortune has always been kept a closely guarded secret. But claims of misdeeds in the Roaring Twenties have never been denied.

Whatever the source of his wealth, Joe was determined to be a winner and his activities amassed a fortune. Even now the family is still raking it in from a lucrative distribution deal struck fifty years ago which gave Joe the exclusive right to import spirits to the States. The deal still stands.

At the age of twenty-one, Joe borrowed money from friends to buy and

Above: The Kennedy brothers: (from left) Robert, Edward and John. Robert and John would both be assassinated. Edward would have his presidential ambitions thwarted by the scandal of Chappaquiddick.

Opposite: Campaigning for election to the American Presidency, John F. Kennedy received rousing adulation wherever he went as he preached his new vision of politics.

Left: The Kennedy Clan of the 1930s....Joseph Kennedy with his wife and eight of their nine children.

sell property and companies. He made killing after killing on the Stock Exchange. By twenty-five he was a bank president and by thirty-five he was a multi-millionaire.

Wealth also brought power, and he was appointed US ambassador to Britain. But the family's strong Irish roots and staunch Catholicism were pointers to a simmering dislike of the British. He opposed US entry into World War II and in 1940 told a reporter: 'Democracy is finished in Britain. The country will go socialist. If the US gets into the war with England, we'll be left holding the bag.' The remark forced him to resign his prestigious title of 'Ambassador to the Court of St James' and he was recalled to Washington with his tail between his legs.

Joe Kennedy swore he would be a millionaire by thirty-five, but by that age he had done so many times over

---

In his quest for power Joe had married Rose Fitzgerald, the daughter of Boston's first Irish mayor. Born into a rich socialite family in 1890, Rose was, in her own way, just as remarkable as Joe.

She married in 1914 and had nine children. She offered her children financial inducements not to smoke or drink until they were twenty-one - a prophetic action in view of their later history of boozing and philandering. She was once quoted as saying: 'I told the boys to study hard, and maybe they'll be President one day.'

Her Irish sympathies were also well known. When she and Joe were invited to spend a weekend as guests of the British royal family at Windsor Castle, she regarded it as a supreme irony, declaring: 'Living well is the best revenge.'

But as well as sharing Joe's political leanings, she also had to share him with other women. During their fifty-five-year marriage he had numerous affairs.

The most famous of his liaisons was with Hollywood star Gloria Swanson. The twenty-nine-year-old actress made all the running in what was to become a two-year affair in the late twenties. Joe handled her business affairs and successfully redirected her career.

Top: *Joseph Kennedy and sons John (left) and Joseph Junior arrive in London for a visit in 1937.*

Above: *Rose Kennedy, surviving matriarch of the Clan and mother of the assassinated John and Robert.*

It was the Catholic Church which ended the affair. In 1929 Gloria was picked up by a Kennedy aide and taken to a hotel room where she was introduced to Cardinal O'Connell, the archbishop of Boston and a friend of the Kennedys.

Extraordinarily, the archbishop told her that Joe had sought his permission either to divorce his wife or to set up a second household with Gloria - recognized and sanctioned by the Church.

O'Connell had declined and now told Gloria: 'I am here to ask you to stop seeing Joseph Kennedy. Each time you see him you become an occasion of sin for him.'

At an extraordinary meeting in a hotel room a Roman Catholic cardinal tried to break up the affair between Joe Kennedy and Gloria Swanson

---

Despite this weird attempt at ending their love affair, the transcontinental trysts continued until 1930 when two events occurred. One was that Gloria Swanson's hard-done-by husband warned he was suing for divorce. The other was that, at a dinner party, Gloria questioned one of Kennedy's business deals involving her career.

Joe exploded in rage, stormed out and flew to Boston, liquidating all his holdings in her movies.

THE CURSE OF THE KENNEDYS

Joseph Kennedy's sons inherited his sexual appetite. They also inherited his Irish republican sympathies. John once declared that his best overseas visit as President had been to Ireland. During his trip he was given a joke 'O'Kennedy' coat of arms. He had it made into a ring seal - but the only time he ever used it was on a letter to the Queen.

The Kennedy fortune is now reckoned to be approaching $1000 million, most of it tied up in trust funds, stocks and shares. But wealth has not saved them from the terrible curse that has dogged the dynasty. The family history is littered with scandal and tragedy.

Joe and Rose's third child, Rosemary, was born mentally retarded and spent most of her life in a home.

In 1944 came the greatest tragedy the family had yet known. Rose and Joe's eldest son, Joe Jr, died at the age of twenty-nine when his bomber blew up over the English Channel. Of all the tragedies that the old man witnessed in his life, the loss of Joe Jr hurt him the most.

Joe had been groomed for greatness by his ambitious father and would probably have been the President that brother John was later to become.

Disaster followed disaster. Four years after Joe Jr's death, Kathleen Kennedy was also killed in a plane crash.

Joe's dream of power was finally fulfilled in 1960 when John F. Kennedy became US President. At least the old man, who died in 1969 at the age of eighty-one, lived to see that proud moment. But tragedy struck again with the assassination of first the President and then brother Robert, the US Attorney-General.

It was only after their deaths that books were written posing questions about Robert's fidelity - and producing solid evidence about the philandering of JFK.

A PRESIDENT ON THE MAKE

In *The Crisis Years* by historian Michael Beschloss, JFK is depicted as a sex-crazy head of state who pursued his romantic pleasures regardless of national security. When he was a twenty-four-year-old naval intelligence officer during World War II, Jack Kennedy supposedly fell madly in love with Danish spy Inga Arvad Fejos, who was at that time working for the Nazis.

The tall, blonde ex-Miss Denmark was under FBI surveillance during their affair, and it almost cost Kennedy his position in the US Navy. It was only the intervention of his father that saved him.

A second shady affair occurred in 1963 when he started seeing Ellen Fimmel Rometsch, a twenty-seven-year-old West German who had been involved with two Communist groups. But when his brother Robert, then Attorney-General, heard of the affair he ordered the poor girl to be expelled from the USA.

Further astonishing evidence of the President's sexual adventures was related in a string of books which revealed his obsessions with film stars Marilyn

Below: *John Kennedy and Jacqueline Bouvier in the society wedding of 1953 at fashionable Newport, Rhode Island.*

Above: *Frank Sinatra, Robert Kennedy and brother-in-law Peter Lawford on their way to a fund-raising dinner in 1961.*

Monroe, Angie Dickinson and Jayne Mansfield. But lesser mortals were also the subjects of JFK's desires.

In the book *A Question of Character: A Life of John F. Kennedy*, Thomas C. Reeves provided evidence of a sex session with a new flame on the President's inauguration night and the hiring of a call girl immediately before Kennedy's famous television face-to-face confrontation with Richard Nixon.

Reeves alleged that CIA informants had told him of proof that JFK liked to get rip-roaring drunk while in the White House - as well as using 'marijuana, cocaine, hashish and acid'.

According to the CIA the President was no stranger to marijuana, cocaine, hashish and acid

---

Two things facilitated the President's astonishing philandering. One was the loyalty of the entire White House staff, including both his and Jackie's secret service guards who would alert him about his wife's movements and give due warning when he needed to break up a sex session.

The other was his friendship with Peter Lawford. Actor Lawford was JFK's

brother-in-law (he had married Jack's sister Pat) and lived in Santa Monica, California, where his beachfront home was headquarters for both Jack and brother Bobby's West Coast expeditions.

MARILYN: USED, ABUSED AND...MURDERED?

It was here that the two were introduced to the movie star Marilyn Monroe. It is generally believed that both brothers had affairs with Marilyn, and that they treated her cynically and dropped her harshly.

Lawford arranged many meetings between JFK and Monroe. When Kennedy won the Democratic presidential nomination he made an acceptance speech at the Los Angeles Coliseum, with Marilyn cheering him on. She then joined the young Kennedy for a skinny-dipping party at Lawford's beach house. Kennedy suddenly decided to stay on in California one extra day.

In May 1962 Jack Kennedy held his forty-fifth birthday party in Madison Square Garden. Marilyn was there at his side. She waddled on to the stage in a skin-tight dress and managed to blurt out a few lines of 'Happy Birthday'. She was scared and drunk. The crowd did not notice, but JFK did. Marilyn Monroe could become an embarrassment. She would have to go.

Soon afterwards poor Marilyn did indeed become an embarrassment. At thirty-six, she was turning more and more to drugs.

The Kennedys realized that, with her diaries and her knowledge of their Californian secret partying, the world's most popular blonde might be believed if she decided to break the presidential code of silence. Word was got to Marilyn that she must not attempt to contact either Bobby or Jack ever again.

It was enough to send the unstable movie star over the edge.

On the morning of 5 August, 1962, Marilyn was found dead at her home in Brentwood, Los Angeles. Did she, as the inquest found, die by her own hand? Was it accident or suicide - or murder?

Rumours of her affairs with Jack and Bobby Kennedy soon swept the world. According to one of her closest friends,

Robert Slatzer, Marilyn had two important meetings planned for the day following her death. One was with her lawyer; the other was a press conference.

At this conference, said Slatzer, Marilyn was going to reveal the truth about her love sessions with the President, or with the Attorney-General, or both. She felt that the brothers had used her, then abandoned her. The only thing that would have stopped her

Left: *Marilyn Monroe was the sex symbol of her age - and the plaything of the Kennedys.*

Below: *The bed on which a legend died. Marilyn Monroe's body was found sprawled across it. Was it accident, suicide or murder?*

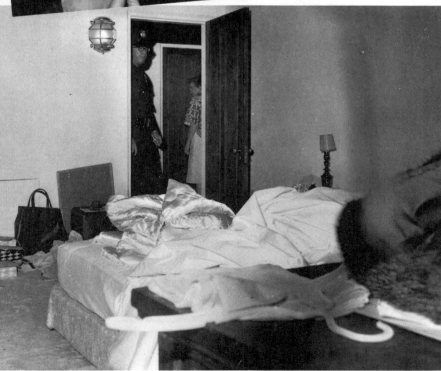

revelations would have been a phone call or a visit from Robert Kennedy on the night of 4 August - her last day on earth.

That night a dinner party had been planned at the home of Peter Lawford. It was rumoured that Robert Kennedy was due to turn up. He never did. Nor did Marilyn. According to Lawford at the inquest, Marilyn told him on the phone she felt too tired.

At a press conference the day after her death Marilyn planned to tell all about her relationship with the Kennedy brothers

---

The theories that Marilyn Monroe had been silenced grew stronger. It was said that her house had been bugged by Robert Kennedy and by the FBI.

Monroe was believed to have had an abortion about this time, and the baby could have been Bobby Kennedy's. Marilyn had tried to contact him at the Justice Department in Washington on numerous occasions in the weeks before her death. The horrifying theory that secret agents killed Marilyn to protect the Kennedy brothers from disgrace was advanced by several authors.

Weird theories indeed. And not far removed from another well-recorded and fully admitted scandal, involving the President and a Mafia gangster's moll...

SHARING A MISTRESS WITH THE MAFIA

After JFK's death word leaked out of affairs that the President had conducted with secretaries, prostitutes, socialites, starlets, movie actresses, journalists and family friends. But no revelation caused more shock than the news in 1975 that Jack Kennedy had kept secret a two-year romance with a dark-haired, blue-eyed beauty called Judith Campbell Exner.

The affair was revealed when a Senate committee began investigating links between the CIA and the attempted overthrow of Cuban leader Fidel Castro. Those links led to Chicago Mafia boss Sam 'Momo' Giancana and his mobster friend Johnny Roselli...and still further down the chain of intrigue to Giancana's girlfriend Judith Campbell Exner. In secret testimony she revealed not only her affair with Giancana but, unexpectedly, another at the same time with Jack Kennedy.

Judith claimed that she was Kennedy's link with the Mafia for most of 1960 and 1961, regularly carrying sealed packages between the President and her two Mafia bosses, Giancana and Roselli.

Exner said she was introduced to Jack Kennedy by Frank Sinatra

---

In her autobiography, *My Story*, Exner said she was introduced to Jack Kennedy in 1960 by singer Frank Sinatra at a Las Vegas party. Kennedy, who was then a Massachusetts senator, said their affair began almost immediately and continued across America, including Chicago, Los Angeles, Palm Beach and Washington.

Below: Presidents past and present...John Kennedy with Dwight Eisenhower at the White House in 1962.

One version of how the affair ended appeared in later reports from FBI sources. Exner, it seemed, had revealed that there had been many telephone calls between the President and FBI director J. Edgar Hoover.

What she may not have known was that some of them were warnings from Hoover to Kennedy that his continued liaison with Exner could destroy him.

A WRONG TURNING AT CHAPPAQUIDDICK

Youngest brother Senator Edward 'Teddy' Kennedy lost his chance of making the presidency when he took a wrong turn on Chappaquiddick Island, off the Cape Cod coast, on Friday night, 18 July 1969.

The thirty-seven-year-old Kennedy had looked as if he would put the family back on the political map as he gained in prestige as Democratic senator for Massachusetts. But the wrong turning he took proved also to be the turning point of his career.

Teddy Kennedy had spent the day sailing with friends before dropping in for a beer at a hotel in Edgartown Harbour. There he was joined by a party of friends, including his cousin Joe Gargan and lawyer Paul Markham.

As evening fell the three men took the short ferry ride across to the island of Chappaquiddick where a party was planned at a secluded, rented cottage. By 8.30 that night they had joined up with three other men and six young women.

Among the guests was Mary Jo Kopechne, at twenty-nine one of the 'boiler room girls' who had worked for Teddy's brother Bobby before his assassination the previous year. What happened as the night wore on may never be fully known...for the senator's recollection of events proved later to be strangely hazy.

Teddy Kennedy said he left the party shortly before midnight to return to Edgartown. He took with him Mary Jo, who had been staying at Edgartown's Dunes Hotel.

The route back to the ferry would have taken Kennedy down Main Street. He knew the road well. Yet Kennedy did not drive down Main Street. Instead of turning left at the crossroads just half a mile from the cottage, he turned sharp right - into Dyke Road and towards the beach.

His black 1967 Oldsmobile car began to cross the 85ft wooden, hump-backed Dyke Bridge, but midway the vehicle plunged off the side into the strong currents of Poucha Pond. A few seconds later, Kennedy emerged gasping for air. He crawled to the safety of the shore.

Later he was to recall that he dived repeatedly in an effort to reach Mary Jo, who was trapped inside the car.

Finally, exhausted and in a state of shock, he rested for fifteen minutes on the beach. Then he started running back towards the cottage where the barbecue was still in progress. He was never able to explain why he did not stop to raise the alarm at a house only two hundred yards away from Dyke bridge.

Instead the senator staggered back to the cottage and, dripping wet in the darkness, called Gargan and Markham outside to talk to him. Softly he told his two friends what had occurred.

Again, there was no attempt to reach a telephone - there being none at the cottage - to call the police and the fire service. The three men chose instead to drive back to the bridge and dive once more to the sunken car in an attempt to recover Mary Jo's body. In despair at having failed to reach her, the three men drove off, leaving behind Mary Jo almost certainly dead - but just possibly trapped in an air pocket and still struggling for life.

Edward Kennedy left the scene of the accident without raising the alarm at a nearby house

---

Further clues to the character of the man who might have been President then emerged. He told Gargan and Markham that he did not want the others to know of Mary Jo's death.

At Teddy's request, his two friends then drove him back through the crossroads, this time taking the correct turning to the ferry landing where again he shunned the use of a telephone. Instead he dived into the water and swam across the channel to the Edgartown side.

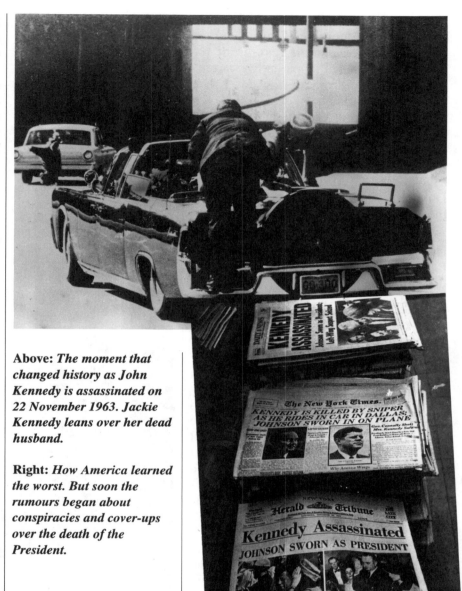

Above: *The moment that changed history as John Kennedy is assassinated on 22 November 1963. Jackie Kennedy leans over her dead husband.*

Right: *How America learned the worst. But soon the rumours began about conspiracies and cover-ups over the death of the President.*

Gargan and Markham said they assumed he had gone to raise the alarm and they drove back to the party.

On the Martha's Vineyard side of the channel, Kennedy was acting out another strange drama. He slipped silently out of the water and crept to his previously booked hotel room at the Shire Inn, in Edgartown, where he changed into fresh, dry clothes. He then wandered outside until he was noticed by the hotel's owner, who was working late.

Kennedy told him: 'I have been asleep. Something woke me up.' Then: 'I seem to have misplaced my watch. Can you tell me what time it is?' It was 2.25am. Kennedy thanked the hotel boss, bade him goodnight and went back into his room. The following morning Kennedy turned up in the hotel's small restaurant for breakfast at 7.30am, apparently none the worse for his ordeal. An hour after that, Gargan and Markham arrived.

According to testimony later, it was at this time that the group belatedly tried to ring a lawyer to report the accident. But Kennedy's Oldsmobile had already been discovered. Edgartown police chief Dominick Arena and his men had taken the ferry to Chappaquiddick.

His two men friends drove him to the ferry landing, where he slipped into the water and swam across to his hotel

---

At the bridge, Arena noted the skid marks and the Oldsmobile appearing above the ebbing tide. The tenant of the nearby house told him she had heard a car drive past around midnight.

Arena borrowed swimming trunks and a face mask and dived down to the car to see if there was a body inside but the 6ft 4in cop found that the strong current made the task too dangerous. He called up divers and radioed his headquarters with the number of the car, L78 207. The reply came back soon afterwards: 'It is registered to Senator Edward Kennedy.'

When diver John Farrar arrived from Edgartown, he examined the car. The driver's window was rolled completely down, the passenger's was fully closed, and the rear window was shattered. In the rear seat he found a girl's body.

In her handbag were keys to an Edgartown motel room, some cosmetics, dollars and a US Senate pass in the name of Rosemary Keogh - a friend. The police concluded that it was Rosemary and not Mary Jo whose body lay in the car.

Meanwhile, Arena received another radio message. Teddy Kennedy was sitting in Edgartown police station waiting to see him. Back in town Arena questioned Kennedy, but his replies were brief and elusive. He sat down and made a written statement.

He claimed that he had been unfamiliar with the route he had taken the night before and described how the car 'went off the side of the bridge'. He went on:

Below: Senator Edward Kennedy's career almost ended in the murky waters of Chappaquiddick Island when Mary Jo Kopechne died in his car in 1969.

Bottom: The turbulent marriage of Edward and Joan Kennedy meant strained moments in public for the feuding celebrity couple.

I attempted to open the door and window of the car but have no recollection of how I got out of the car. I came to the surface and then repeatedly dove down to the car in an attempt to see if the passenger was still in the car. I was unsuccessful in the attempt. I was exhausted and in a state of shock. I recall walking back to where my friends were eating. There was a car in front of the cottage and I climbed into the back seat. I then asked for someone to bring me back to Edgartown. I remember walking around for a period of time and then going back to my hotel room. When I fully realized what had happened this morning I immediately contacted the police.

Kennedy's curious police statement left so many questions unanswered that he was immediately assumed to be hiding his guilt

---

The statement left so many questions unanswered that a presumption of guilt was natural.

Meanwhile, the Kennedy machine swept into action to tidy up the rotten affair. Mary Jo's body was flown to

Pennsylvania in a plane chartered by the senator. He himself hid away at his nearby home at Hyannis Port.

Four days after Mary Jo's death, Kennedy flew to Pennsylvania to attend her funeral at St Vincent's Roman Catholic church. He was accompanied by his pregnant wife Joan and by his brother Bobby's widow Ethel. Kennedy surprised mourners by appearing at the funeral in a neck brace - worn, he said, because of injuries suffered in the accident.

Three days later he returned to Martha's Vineyard to plead guilty to the minor charge of leaving the scene of an accident. He was given a suspended two-month jail sentence and banned from driving for a year.

Kennedy's guilty plea saved him the embarrassment of giving evidence at the hearing. But it failed to silence press disquiet about what was seen as a cover-up. Kennedy was impelled to go on nationwide television and make a long, yet still evasive statement about the Chappaquiddick tragedy.

Kennedy's rambling apologia on TV made Life magazine accuse him of hustling heart-strings and trading on Kennedy credibility

---

He tried to 'explain' his strange actions after his car crashed into the water:

All kinds of scrambled thoughts ...went through my mind during this period. They were reflected in the various, inexplicable, inconsistent and inconclusive things I said and did, including such questions as whether the girl might still be alive somewhere out of that immediate area, whether some awful curse did actually hang over all the Kennedys... I was overcome, I'm frank to say, by a jumble of emotions - grief, fear, doubt, exhaustion, panic, confusion and shock.

And so on, ending with an equally rambling plea to be allowed to remain senator for Massachusetts.

He remained a senator, but his hopes of ultimate power died with Mary Jo Kopechne. Over the years Kennedy languished in a political pool flanked by bouts of boozing and womanizing.

His marriage to wife Joan ended in divorce in 1983. And tales of the senator canoodling with various young ladies in different parts of the globe became stock in trade for the popular tabloids.

CONTINUING THE FAMILY LEGEND

While Teddy hit the high spots, other Kennedy clan scandals continued. In 1983, Robert Kennedy Jr was arrested for possessing heroin. Shortly afterwards, brother David, twenty-eight, died of a drugs overdose in a seedy Florida motel room after a week of heavy partying. Cousin Teddy Jr fought cancer and had a leg amputated, only to be arrested a few years later for possessing drugs.

And in 1991 Edward Kennedy's nephew, William Kennedy Smith, was arrested over allegations that he had raped a woman at the Kennedy family mansion in Palm Beach.

After this latest shock a US poll revealed that the Kennedy name had by then become associated more with scandal and debauchery than with charitable or political achievements. But given patriarch Joseph Sr's beginnings in the bootlegging twenties, it is perhaps only reasonable to ask: had the Kennedy clan's reputation done any more than come full circle?

Below: *William Kennedy Smith listens in court to evidence about his alleged sex attack on a girl he invited back to the family's Palm Beach home.*

ELVIS – THE KING
The Death of a Legend

To millions of fans Elvis Presley was – and still is – the King. He was also an obese, violent drug addict with bizarre sexual tastes. What made him what he was?

His adoring fans see him as the all American boy, devoted son, model army recruit, generous friend and gifted entertainer. Others knew Elvis Aron Presley as an obese, violent monster, obsessed with death and kinky sex, a drug addict who popped pills by the bucketful to hide from the real world.

But all agree that he was the King.

He had it all. Fans, fame, fortune and an unmatchable talent. But he died aged only forty-two, grossly overweight, with an amazing total of thirteen drugs in his bloodstream. He took pills to go to sleep. He took pills to get up. He took pills to go to the lavatory and he took pills to stop him from going to the lavatory.

And he was in the bathroom when he

fell on to the thickly carpeted floor after a massive heart attack. Despite bodyguards, a live-in fiancee and a thousand so-called friends he lay there alone and cold for three hours before he was discovered. The King was dead. But who was the King?

At the autopsy a total of thirteen drugs were found in his bloodstream

---

In the last years of his life Elvis had become a bloated parody of the handsome, clean-living, pelvis-swinging star who had earned a billion dollars and was the idol of the world.

As his ex-wife Priscilla said, 'He became crazed with inactivity and boredom.' Night had become day for Elvis: he slept through the daylight hours and stayed up all night.

Above: *Elvis, Priscilla and their baby daughter, Lisa Marie - born on the 2 February 1968.*

Opposite: *Bloated and dependant on drugs to get him on stage, Elvis Presley ended his singing career as a sad shambling figure.*

Left: *Fresh-faced and youthful, Elvis at the start of his career and on the trail to international superstardom in the Fifties.*

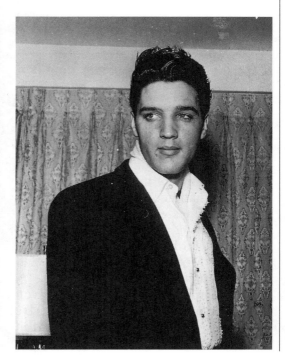

His sex-life became perverted. He was a voyeur, installing two-way mirrors in rooms through which he could secretly watch his friends engage in sexual acts with girls. He used video equipment to tape his own sex movies, some of lesbian activities.

But it was his drug addiction that killed him. Whenever he arrived in a new town he would send out his aides to find doctors to prescribe the huge daily doses of pills that he needed. Stepbrother David Stanley remembers what happened when the aides failed in Las Vegas:

He jumped on a table, pulled out his gun and said, 'I'll buy a goddam drug store if I want to. I'm going to get what I want. You people had better realize that either you're with me or you're against.

His concerts had become farces. Under the influence of drugs he forgot the words of numbers he had sung for years. He would ramble on incoherently to the audience. Hundreds walked out of a Las Vegas concert because he spent half-an-hour giving a karate demonstration.

It had been a sad decline for the ex-truck driver who, slim and sexy, had led a revolution in music twenty years earlier.

ADORED AND SPOILT

He was born on 8 January 1935 in East Tupelo, Mississippi, the only child of Gladys and Vernon Presley. Gladys, a sewing machine operator, knew she had been carrying twins but her doctor did not believe her. So when Elvis was delivered the doctor turned away and began cleaning up. Gladys was still in pain - a labour pain. A few minutes later Elvis's twin brother, Jesse Aron, was born dead.

His over-protective mother insisted on accompanying Elvis to and from school almost up to the day he left

---

Elvis always shared a close relationship with his mother. Gladys was over-protective of the spoilt young boy, taking him everywhere she went. He slept in her bed during his early years.

When Elvis started school, Gladys always insisted on walking him there and bringing him home in the afternoon. This daily ritual lasted almost to the end of

Above: *Elvis at 27 fishing in the Pacific waters of Hawaii during a break in the making of his film* **Girls, Girls, Girls.**

Below: *Presley's smouldering looks and singing talents at the height of his stardom in 1962.*

Elvis's schooldays and caused him a great deal of embarrassment. Finally, he insisted she should walk behind him and on the other side of the road, hidden by the bushes if possible.

MUSICAL BEGINNINGS

Vernon Presley, who did any jobs that came up, regularly attended the Assembly of God church with his wife. It was there that Elvis heard music - and sang - for the first time.

He won his first award for singing at a county fair. The young boy was placed second and won $5.

Given the choice, Elvis would have preferred the rifle - but since Gladys was paying it had to be the guitar

---

It was Gladys who went with Elvis to buy his first real guitar. It replaced the home-made model made from a lard can that Elvis had acquired in a swap with another youngster. When Elvis and his mother arrived at the hardware store, though, the birthday boy had his heart set on a rifle. Mother did not approve - and in the end prevailed.

When he was twelve, he was given encouragement by his teacher, Mrs Camp. She asked her class to take part in a talent show. Elvis, a new boy, shyly put up his hand and said he could sing a little and play the guitar. Next day he turned up with his guitar and sang his favourite song, 'Old Shep'. From then on he took his guitar to school every day.

The family moved to Memphis but life was always a struggle. In high school he learned to love football - and blues and country music. He began to wear his hair long and grew his famous side-burns for the first time. And he began to perform publicly for the first time. He would play at school and at the local boys' clubs.

Already there was no shortage of girls attracted to the shy, heavy-lidded, handsome young man. He fell in love for the first time - with a pretty fifteen-year-old called Dixie Locke. His parents even thought marriage was a possibility.

Once his schooldays were behind him - he was an average pupil - he got a job truck-driving for $41 a week. His route often took him past the Memphis Recording Studio, where you could make your own record for $4.

One Saturday in July 1953 Elvis took time off and turned up at the studio to cut two songs as a present for his mother. 'Who do you sound like?' asked the assistant Marion Keisker. 'I don't sound like nobody,' he replied. How right he was.

He recorded the two Ink Spots numbers 'My Happiness' and 'That's When Your Heartaches Begin' and made a big impression on Marion. She remembered him and constantly badgered her boss, Sam Phillips, about the teenager.

But it was a year before Phillips fixed up a recording session for Elvis. On 5 July 1954 he made the single 'That's All Right, Mama'. Two days later, a local radio disc jockey played the record fourteen times in a row.

'I don't sound like nobody,' said the young Elvis when he arrived at the recording studio - and indeed he was right

---

It was another case of a woman being a big influence in Elvis's life. He said later: 'If it wasn't for Marion I would never have got a start. That woman, she was the one who had faith, she was the one who pushed me. Sure, Sam had the studio - but it was Marion who did it for me.'

The first record order was for five thousand discs, and it climbed to number three in the Memphis country and western charts. Elvis and his group the Starlight Wranglers - later renamed the Blue Moon Boys - were in demand. Their second record didn't sell so well, but then along came Colonel Tom Parker.

ENTER COLONEL PARKER

He told the naïve youngster: 'You stay talented and sexy and I'll make amazing deals that'll make us both as rich as rajahs. Parker was a wheeler-dealer in the carnival/show-business world and he was telling the truth. The Colonel owned Elvis till the singer died: and he took 50 per cent of every dollar that Elvis earned.

It was Colonel Tom who insisted that Elvis developed his hip-wiggling style. And in Jacksonville, Florida he realized that he'd hit gold. It was there that

Below: *Elvis Presley and Frank Sinatra on the set of the 1965 movie* **Frankie and Johnny.**

Above: *Elvis married only once - to Priscilla. The couple later divorced but she kept his name.*

teenagers for the first time tried to rip off Elvis's clothes. He had become a sex star.

But one girl who was not impressed was girlfriend Dixie. When Elvis's career began to take off and he was spending weeks on the road, she found she wanted more than just loving phone calls. It broke his heart when she left him after eighteen months and married someone else.

Colonel Parker promised to make them both as rich as rajahs - no idle boast since he took a cool 50 per cent

---

Elvis's first appearance on network television in 1956 changed him into a national sensation. The older generation were repelled by Presley's mean, sexy image. He was attacked from pulpits and in editorial columns, and banned from radio programmes.

The teenagers, on the other hand, loved it all - particularly because their parents hated everything he stood for. Reluctantly show business had to accept him. After all, he was the country's No.1 recording star after 'Heartbreak Hotel' had sold a million.

He was already the King, Elvis the Pelvis or the Guitar-Playing Brando. There were Presley jeans, charm bracelets, guitars, T-shirts, bobbysocks, bermuda shorts. Presley was only twenty-one and already a millionaire.

GOODBYE TO GLADYS

In 1956, as well as 'Heartbreak Hotel', he released 'Hound Dog', 'Don't Be Cruel', 'Blue Suede Shoes' and 'Love Me Tender'. *Love me Tender* was the title of the first film he made with 20th-Century Fox. The record sold over 2 million copies.

In 1957 Elvis purchased Graceland, his home for the last twenty years of his life. He paid $100,000 for the building which had been previously used as a church. The two-storey mansion contained twenty-three rooms. He painted it blue and gold so that it glowed in the dark. And Mom and Dad moved in.

The fans may have wanted Elvis - but so did the US Army. In December 1957 he was drafted for two years. Elvis said he was quite prepared to 'do his share' and 'to protect his country'.

While doing his military service in Texas his beloved mother became ill. She returned to Memphis and was admitted to hospital where she was diagnosed as having 'acute severe hepatitis'. As days passed she sank lower while Elvis fought with the Army for a leave pass. At last they gave it, and he fought his way through the crowds to her bedside.

She died a few days later at the age of forty-six. Elvis was distraught. Vernon was there at her death and rang Elvis at Graceland. At the graveside Elvis collapsed several times. He leaned on the casket, weeping, and said, 'Oh God, everything I have is gone. Goodbye darling, goodbye, goodbye.'

Elvis never got over his mother's death, and his obsession with her prevented him from ever achieving emotional maturity

---

He was never to recover from the trauma. Author Albert Goldman described his relationship with his mother in these words:

Elvis's obsession with his mother lasted throughout his life, even though she died several years before he did. It was an unnatural obsession that ...certainly accounts for many of Elvis's later sexual problems.

It was a suffocating relationship that never really gave Elvis the chance to grow up a man.

THE SLIDE INTO SEX AND DRUGS

He left for Germany with the Army a few weeks later. It was while serving in Europe that stories of his sexual excesses began to emerge. His wild lifestyle began, says Goldman, in Paris in 1959 when he discovered the Lido nightclub and the Bluebell Girls' chorus line.

For two weeks Presley ate dinner at the club and then took the entire chorus line back to his hotel. 'He toyed with them till dawn,' he reports. And it was while he

Above: *Elvis was once a truck driver on $41 a week. His route took him past the Memphis record studios where he found fame.*

Below: *Surprisingly Elvis Presley did not make London's Madame Tussauds waxworks exhibition until 1978. He stood in the Hall of Heroes.*

was serving in Germany that Elvis started popping pills for the first time.

He came back from two years' service having found a bride, Priscilla (although they didn't marry for another seven years), to find that the world still clamoured for him. Parker had done a good job while Elvis had been serving his country.

From the spring of 1961 to the summer of 1968 Elvis made twenty-one films and about $5 million. He worked and played hard. And he turned to pills for support.

Colonel Parker was nothing if not efficient. After two years as a GI Elvis went on to make twenty-one films and $5 million

---

In Hollywood, Colonel Parker set up Elvis and his bodyguards - dubbed the Memphis Mafia - in a Bel Air mansion which had belonged to Aly Khan and Rita Hayworth. 'It became the head-quarters for the most intently partying group of bachelors in the history of Hollywood,' wrote Goldman.

The parties...would commence every night at about ten. The basic idea was to fill the house with attractive young women who had been specially selected to conform to Elvis's exacting criteria.

Elvis liked small, kittenish girls who were built to his ideal proportions. They were to be no higher than 5 ft 2 in and weigh no more than 110 lbs. What was critical was that the girls be as young as possible, certainly no older than eighteen, and that they be not too far removed from the condition of virginity. Elvis liked to see a pretty girl dressed all in white. White panties were Elvis's erotic fetish.

Elvis the nice guy was forgotten. He was turning into an arrogant, bad-tempered bore who insisted on respect and blind obedience. Elvis's trigger-sharp temper exploded into violence more than once against a girl who dared to answer back. He threw things at them like a hysterical woman - once a water melon; another time, more dangerously, a knife.

Once Elvis had made his way into the master bedroom with the pick of the litter, the Mafia were free to enjoy the remainder. While they did what comes naturally, Elvis was mostly content to watch his group of girls strip down to their panties and wrestle.

For fun Elvis had a 40 lb, 4 ft tall alcoholic chimp called Scatter who joined in the wrestling and was great for practical jokes. He once climbed up the drainpipe to the second-floor office of Sam Goldwyn. As he came swinging through the window, Goldwyn's secretary ran screaming in horror from the room. Scatter then enraged the legendary producer by leaping on to his desk.

Elvis bought one of the first home video cameras, and with co-operative young women made his own endless series of bedroom follies.

Elvis's alcoholic pet chimpanzee once shinned up a drainpipe and broke into Sam Goldwyn's office

---

But at the same time as these tacky bedroom antics, he was wooing the co-stars of his movies: Tuesday Weld, Ursula Andress, Yvonne Craig and Ann-Margret. He also dated Natalie Wood.

Elvis liked film work, but got more and more depressed as the films he made got cheaper and cheaper.

And so he turned to pills more and more. He ran a football club called Elvis Presley Enterprises. Everyone in the team would take two uppers. They then played four or five games straight off, said ex-bodyguard Red West. After the uppers came painkillers for the injuries. Inexorably the King was becoming a walking chemist's shop.

Musically, the mid-1960s was a period of decline for Elvis. His singles did not reach number one. There was more competition, especially from Britain and the Beatles.

MARRIAGE - AND DIVORCE

On 1 May 1967 the singer at last married Priscilla Ann Beaulieu, whom he always called Cilla. They had met when she was fourteen. Priscilla's stepfather was a captain in the US Air Force stationed with his family in Germany at the same time that Elvis was in the Army.

Priscilla was invited to Graceland for Christmas 1960 and then returned to

Above: *Hundreds of statuettes of the King were turned out every month by the Zsolnay porcelain works in Hungary.*

Below: *A bronze statue of Elvis got a public airing in London in 1981. It was valued at £25,000.*

Germany. Missing her, Elvis called her stepfather, and asked if she could finish her schooling in Memphis under his watchful eye. A year later he agreed, and she moved into Graceland in October 1962.

Elvis had proposed to Priscilla when she turned twenty-one on the insistence of Colonel Tom Parker. They married in Las Vegas and honeymooned in Palm Springs, California. They then moved into the West Coast Graceland in Beverly Hills. Nine months later their only child, Lisa Marie, was born.

Professionally, marriage gave Elvis new impetus. But in his private life he continued womanizing as before

---

Elvis slimmed down his staff, but that was the only change that the newly-wed star made to his personal life. His pill-popping continued at a destructive rate - as did his womanizing.

And author Albert Goldman says it was not long after the birth of Lisa Marie that Priscilla, fed up with Elvis's behaviour, got involved with another man: Elvis's friend and karate coach handsome Mike Stone.

But professionally, marriage seemed to give Elvis new impetus. He moved out of films and started recording and giving live shows again. On 31 July 1969 he started a sensational one-month engagement at the International Hotel in Las Vegas. He broke all attendance records: 161,500 people saw his show.

Touring again, he needed the amphetamines more than ever to call on his reserves of energy. As he put on weight, he took uppers to kill his appetite. Former body-guard Rick Stanley said: 'There were no half-measures. In 1972-73 he started getting into needles. That's when I really started to worry when he became a needle head. His body began to look like a pin cushion.'

Elvis was a stranger to moderation - once he started to inject his drugs his body quickly resembled a pincushion

---

Everything seemed to be booming for Elvis in the early 1970s. But the long tours of one-night stands brought him no great sense of fulfilment, although they did bring lots of cash. In 1974 he earned

Below: *Elvis in the film* **Change of Habit,** *in which he played a doctor who falls in love with a nurse.*

himself over $7 million gross. Of course he had to pay Colonel Tom his regular 50 per cent, but Elvis had a bizarre and extravagant life-style.

He bought fourteen Cadillacs in one night in Memphis and gave them away to friends, and then invited in an old Negro woman who happened to be passing to pick any car she fancied.

Said his old friend Jerry Shering: 'He still was not content. He loved performing live before a public, he liked being Elvis Presley and the adulation...'

In 1972 Priscilla could not take any more. Her affair with Mike Stone came out in the open. Elvis's drug-addled mind turned to murder. Says Goldman: 'When Priscilla finally asked for a divorce, Elvis was shattered. It wasn't so much the divorce itself, more devastation to his pride, the fact that the world could see that he was being rejected.'

Elvis sued for divorce and it was granted on 18 August 1973. When she told him that she was leaving, Priscilla explained to him: 'It's not that you've lost me for another man. You've lost me to a life of my own.' She was to go on to find stardom in the TV soap *Dallas*.

THE DRUGS TAKE OVER

As Elvis passed forty in January 1975 he literally ballooned. Living on a diet of junk food he lost control of his weight. He'd lost control of his drug-taking a long time before. He called it medication.

Nine days after his divorce came through he was admitted to the Baptist Memorial Hospital, officially for hypertension and headaches but in fact to be dried out.

At one time, Elvis was buying $4,000 worth of pills at a time. But his adoring public had no clue of his addiction until Elvis's father sacked bodyguards Sonny West, his cousin Red West and David Hebler. They co-authored a book called: *Elvis, What Happened?*

Published in 1977 just two weeks before his death, it revealed the full, shocking truth that had been hidden from the public for years. Said Hebler: 'No one forced the pills down Elvis's throat. It was the other way round...He was far from an unwilling victim. He demanded drugs and he used pressure to get them.'

He was now sinking into a life of total debauchery. He ate only hamburgers, he was grotesquely heavy, and his last concerts were farcical. But the fans still loved him. Robert Hilburn of the *Los Angeles Times* wrote:

Blinded by love, cheered - instead of hooted - he strutted across the stage night after night in Las Vegas and in countless other cities in a glittery cape, 50 lb overweight and barely able to focus on the business at hand.

Elvis's bodily functions were so impaired by excessive drug-taking that his aides had to put nappies on him

---

Towards the end of 1976, Elvis had a new steady girlfriend - Ginger Alden, a runner-up in the Miss Tennessee beauty pageant. She was nineteen years younger than Elvis, and on 26 January 1977 she alleges they got engaged. Elvis proposed in the bathroom next to their bedroom, and gave her an 11½ carat diamond ring worth $60,000. They were due to be married, she said, on Christmas Day 1977. Elvis was never to make the date.

He was degenerating fast. His hair was dyed, and his mind and body were so mutilated by drugs that he had lost all control of his bodily functions and had to

be wrapped in nappies by his aides. He was regularly taken to hospital, needing treatment for an enlarged colon and a liver infection.

On 15 August 1977 Elvis played in the afternoon with daughter Lisa Marie who was staying for a fortnight's holiday. In the early evening he made an appointment with his dentist for himself and his girlfriend Ginger Alden. At 10.30 pm they arrived at his surgery. Ginger had X-rays, while Elvis had two fillings.

At 2.30 in the morning, after returning to Graceland, he stripped down to play two hours of energetic racquet-ball. At about 6.30am Elvis and Ginger retired to bed. At 9am she awoke briefly to find him still awake. Elvis told her that he was going into the bathroom to read.

Ginger said: 'Don't fall asleep.'

Elvis replied: 'OK, I won't.'

At about 2.20 in the afternoon she awoke and found that he had not returned. Calling 'Elvis' and getting no reply, she pushed open the bathroom door and found him on the carpeted floor, as if he had fallen from the black leather lavatory seat on which he had been reading.

His face was a grotesque purple mask. She told a reporter: 'I opened one of his eyes and it was just blood red.'

She called for Joe Esposito, Elvis's tour manager who tried to revive him. In the seven-minute ride to Baptist Memorial Hospital Elvis's personal doctor, Dr Nichopolous, kept on repeating: 'Breathe, Elvis. Come on, breathe. Please.' But it was no good. At 3.30pm Elvis was pronounced dead.

'Basically,' said the coroner, 'it was a natural death.' The illusion had to be preserved

---

Of the total of thirteen drugs found in his bloodstream one was merely an anti-histamine for nasal congestion and three - including morphine - had been created by the reactions of the ten that he had taken.

But within hours of his death the big cover-up started. Elvis's family, his sycophantic cronies, his doctors and Memphis itself were desperate to hide the truth about his last drug-filled hours.

Below: Stepmother Dee Presley shocked the world with her book Elvis We Love You Tender *in 1980.*

Despite the torrent of drugs in his bloodstream the verdict was Natural Death. Dr Jerry Francisco, the Memphis State Medical Examiner, said that death had been caused by an erratic heartbeat - 'cardiac arrythmia'.

It was two years later before the full extent of the cover-up was revealed when Dr 'Nick', who had so desperately tried to bring Elvis back to life, was charged with malpractice.

Tennessee public health inspector Steve Belsky said: 'Elvis Presley, from my experience, was issued more scheduled uppers, downers and amphetamines than any other individual that I have ever seen.'

Throughout the world Elvis's fans went into mourning after his death. Colonel Tom Parker immediately rang the grief-stricken Vernon Presley and made sure that he could continue acting for Elvis's estate. He went on to make Elvis richer in death than in life.

Close friends were allowed to see the bloated figure of Elvis 'lying in state' and hundreds of thousands attended the private funeral service conducted at Graceland. The confusion was so great that two mourners were run over by a car and killed.

The King was finally laid to rest beside the adored mother who was responsible for so much

---

Elvis's body was buried in Forest Hill cemetery, but after a body-snatching attempt and because of the large numbers of fans who came to visit his grave he was brought back to Graceland and laid to rest in the Meditation Gardens beside his beloved mother. On her gravestone Elvis had written: 'She was the sunshine of our home.'

Sex pervert? Drug addict? Narcissistic comic-book macho-man smothered by mother-love? Whatever the shocking truth and hidden secrets of Elvis Aron Presley, no one can ever deny him his title: the King.

Below: *Millions of fans pay homage to Elvis at his grave and the graves of his parents.*

JOYCE McKINNEY
A Story of Obsession

In 1977 the story of Joyce McKinney was Britain's No.1 headline-hitting scandal. Obsessed by a clean-living young Mormon missionary, she chased him across the Atlantic, kidnapped him and bound him in chains while she indulged her erotic passions

An alien visiting Britain in 1977 might have been forgiven for thinking that Joyce McKinney was the most important person on the planet. It was a rare day indeed during the final months of that year when you could buy a newspaper, turn on a radio or TV or walk into a pub and not read, hear, see or talk about the blonde with the infectious smile who had captivated the land.

Above: *Kirk Anderson, the object of Joyce McKinney's bizarre desires carries his Bible out of court in Epsom, Surrey in 1977.*

Opposite: *Joyce McKinney is driven away from court in tears and behind bars, suddenly the most written-about woman of the year.*

Left: *Hippie girl Joyce, the flower-power child, reveals the sensuous side of her character.*

On one day the *Daily Mail*, perhaps sensing that its own readership was suffering from McKinney overkill, ran a headline claiming it was 'the only paper WITHOUT Joyce McKinney'! But it was a short-lived break from the American woman whose lust for a young Mormon missionary called Kirk Anderson held gossip-hungry Britain spellbound.

STRICT UPBRINGING

Joyce McKinney was born in Minneapolis, North Carolina, in August 1950. Her father, Davies, was principal of an elementary school and her mother, Maxine, a former teacher of English there. Little Joyce's life was orderly and strict. She began the day with prayers and ended it the same way, and by the time she was four she could recite huge tracts of the Bible by heart. She attended Christian Bible Camp every summer.

By the time she was four the young Joyce could recite huge tracts of the Bible by heart

Her mother remembers her: 'Joyce had high morals. As she grew older she never smoked, drank or used any kind of drug. And if any boy tried to kiss her she would tell him off in no uncertain way. Never did I think she would blossom from tomboy into beauty queen.'

But blossom she did, and the Joyce McKinney who sang lustily in choir soon found her lust directed towards men. She won a beauty contest and her 38-24-36 figure was soon provoking admiring glances from many red-blooded men.

THE START OF AN OBSESSION

After graduating from the University of North Carolina, with a degree in science she moved to Brigham Young University in Utah, the heartland of the Mormon Church. Having met a Mormon family, Joyce thought she would find her own spiritual fulfilment at the stronghold town of the faith. 'What I found, though, was that I was having to fight guys off all the time to keep my virginity,' she said.

In July 1975 she met the man who was

Above: *Joyce at a London party with wild man of rock Keith Moon, drummer with The Who.*

spot. *I turned to my girlfriend there and then and said: 'Hey, get out - I'm in love!'...He kissed me and it was bombs, firecrackers, the Fourth of July.*

The man was Kirk Anderson, and within two years he would be kidnapped, sexually assaulted by her and forced to testify at one of the strangest criminal proceedings Britain has ever witnessed.

After that first meeting it seems that Joyce became obsessed beyond reason with the young Mormon. They made love and enjoyed dating each other, but there was pressure from the Church that made Anderson end the relationship.

His calling within the Church called for chastity, and he saw his bishop to confess his dilemma. He was advised to break off the affair.

'He kissed me, and it was bombs, firecrackers and the Fourth of July'

He saw Joyce for one last tearful time, and then flew to Britain in 1976 to embark on his work of spreading the word of his Church. Joyce meanwhile flew to Hollywood in a fruitless attempt at breaking into showbusiness.

In Tinsel Town she soon tasted the bitter fruits of frustration and rejection. She moved into an apartment with Steve Moskowitz in October 1976 after meeting him at a Hollywood party. He recalled: 'She looked beautiful and I wondered why she had no man with her. But when we began talking she told me about this guy Kirk Anderson, and I soon realized from the way she was going on about him that there was no other person for her...although I desired her like mad there was nothing sexual between us because of her love for Kirk.'

Moskowitz was perhaps the first person to realize the massive obsession growing inside her for Anderson. He went on:

Her whole life centred around meeting him again and getting him away from the grip of the Mormons. In February 1977 she got 15,000 dollars in compensation for some slight injuries she received in a car crash. She realized that at last she had the money to carry out her plan - to go to England and be with him.

to become her obsession - an obsession that would lead to her amazing collision with the full majesty of British law.

She had bought herself a new Stingray Corvette car and was trying it out around town with her girlfriend. She said:

We had pulled up outside of an ice cream parlour...when a white Corvette with a sandy-haired boy at the wheel pulled in beside us. He got out, came over to my car, and asked to drive. He leaned through the window, and I found myself gazing into the deepest pair of baby-blue eyes. He put Paul Newman to shame. My heart did flip-flops on the

...She told me her first aim in England was to give Kirk 'a sexual experience that he would never forget'. She started building up a collection of porno books and I had to take her to porno movies because she wanted to examine sex techniques.

'I had to take her to porno movies,' said Moskowitz, 'because she wanted to examine sex techniques'

After placing a bizarre ad. in a newspaper asking for a 'muscleman, a pilot and a preacher' to help her in a 'romantic adventure', Joyce teamed up with an impressionable, quiet-spoken trainee architect called Keith May.

May, who was twenty-two when he entered into this extraordinary plot with the twenty-seven-year-old Joyce, later admitted he was besotted with her. He said: 'I was floored by her looks and admit I would have done anything for her. I know she only wanted this Anderson guy, but I secretly hoped she would eventually fall in love with me.'

Joyce told May that Anderson secretly loved her but was unable to break free of the influence of the Mormon church. So she could - with the aid of her newly recruited sidekick - do nothing except break those bonds of the Church herself.

THE CRAZY PLOT UNFOLDS

The couple flew to England where they rented a room at a house in Hendon, North London - the base for her 'mission' for Kirk. On 14 September 1977 the whole twisted plot was set in motion.

The twenty-one-year-old missionary was based at the Church of the Latter Day Saints at Ewell in Surrey. Emerging from the church that evening, he was confronted by Joyce and May - May was brandishing a fake revolver. Later, at a pre-trial hearing McKinney was charged with kidnapping, entering Britain on a false passport and possession of fake firearms. Anderson testified that he was bundled off before awakening the following day in a strange bedroom.

He told Epsom magistrates' court in October of that year:

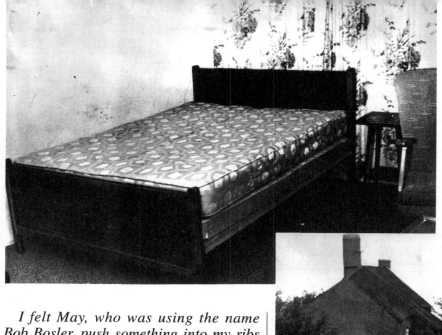

I felt May, who was using the name Bob Bosler, push something into my ribs and he grabbed my shoulder. I was startled and as I looked down I saw it was a gun. I was quite scared. He told me to come with him. I did not know then that the gun was an imitation.

He took me to a car parked about fifty yards away. I got into the rear seat. Joyce was in the front seat wearing a dark wig and she had another gun. I thought that was real too. She said something like how did I think eight thousand miles of ocean was going to keep us apart, or something to that effect. She got into the back seat with me and told me to put my head down. He told her to put a blanket over my head so I could not see where I was going.

Was Kirk Anderson a willing sex slave, or a rape victim in fur-lined manacles?

When I was allowed to remove the blanket I saw I was inside a garage and I was taken to a house adjoining it. I had no idea where I was. I was taken to the bedroom and allowed to sit while Joyce cooked some dinner...She told me she still loved me and wanted to marry me. She said I could be there for two or three months and she said she intended that we could just be together from that time onward. I spent that night with Joyce in the same room although nothing of a physical nature took place...The next day Bob Bosler - Keith May - placed a leather strap attached to a chain on my leg and he attached the chain to the bed. It was about ten foot long so I could in fact move off the bed but not very far. He said he had to chain me for her

Top: *The bed where Joyce's alleged sexual assault on the manacled missionary took place.*

Above: *The holiday cottage of Lower Holstock Farm, Devon where bespectacled Mormon Kirk Anderson was held.*

For the next ninety-six hours Kirk Anderson was either a willing sex slave to Joyce McKinney - or the prisoner of an obsessed woman who bound him in fur-lined manacles before ripping off his 'chastity vest' to force herself upon him.

The case ended up before Epsom magistrates' court because Anderson eventually escaped.

REVELATIONS IN COURT

The normally staid court was used to hearing speeding offences and burglaries - not the excitable outpourings of a woman who, as she told them, 'would have skied down Everest, backwards, with a carnation up my nose for him.'

During the committal proceedings

Above: *Joyce McKinney begs onlookers to pray for her as she is dragged from a prison van into cells at Epsom magistrates' court.*

journalists filled notebook after notebook with the lurid allegations. Anderson told how she manacled him and performed oral sex on him, how she begged him to marry her and how she dressed up in kinky clothes. She said she did it all for him.

When McKinney took the stand there were even more shocks in store. She said she had been made pregnant by the young missionary the first time they had met, but that she had miscarried.

In court McKinney described the kidnapping of Anderson as 'three days of fun, food and sex'

Describing the cottage affair as nothing more than 'three days of fun, food and sex', she went on:

My standards were quite high...I don't smoke, drink or use drugs. I wanted

someone who could read the Bible with me and have a family with me. I prayed for a very special boy to come into my life - and that is where Kirk comes in.

He was afraid of excommunication from the Church and that is why all these lies are coming in...

How could an eight-stone girl rape an eighteen-stone six-foot-two-inch man? His legs are as big round as my waist. Kirk wanted a holiday from his mission, with sex and food, but he had to go back and face his Church president. Kirk says I tempted him. He told Epsom police I was wearing a skin-tight leopard-skin jump-suit. I had black jeans with a scruffy-sleeved top - which has about as much sex appeal as a potato sack.

Referring to the bonds which secured him to the bed, McKinney said matter-of-factly that he had a hang-up about sex, and could not be satisfied until he was chained up.

THE LADY VANISHES

After two weeks it was decided that there was enough evidence to press for a full criminal trial for McKinney and May. But by granting them bail the magistrates ensured that they would never be seen in Britain again.

The trial was set at the Old Bailey for 2 May, but in April - posing as nuns - McKinney and May fled to Eire and from there to Toronto and New York. They kept up their disguises until she was back in North Carolina. A storm of protest followed their vanishing act in England. There was bitter criticism of the bail system which allowed them to go free, and of inadequate immigration checks.

But since they had been dressed as nuns - and convincing nuns at that - there seemed little point in initiating a witch-hunt among the authorities.

A year later, in July 1979, she and May were tracked down to a caravan park in North Carolina by an FBI special agent, and they were charged with making false passport applications. But there was no attempt to bring them back to England.

Joyce received a £700 fine for her false passport application, and resurfaced in the news five years later when she was arrested outside the Salt Lake City, Utah, workplace of her unrequited love Anderson. She was ordered to undergo psychiatric tests but said: 'I love him...I will always love him.'

The world of scandal awaits to see what her next move will be.

Left: *Joyce celebrates her freedom with her parents. She slipped out of England dressed as a nun.*

Below: *Joyce McKinney's creed was: 'I believe you should give a man what he wants. What Kirk wanted I was willing to do.'*

ROCK HUDSON
A Secret Life

The hunky heart-throb screen star was gay, but kept his double life secret from his fans for decades. When Rock Hudson got AIDS, however, the truth could be concealed no longer

Just a few months after he had been forced to admit his innermost secret to a stunned world, Rock Hudson, the most dashing silver screen hero of his time, succumbed to AIDS at his stately Beverly Hills home. It was 2 October 1985 - and the day he died.

For almost forty years his fans had revered him as an indestructible, manly love god coveted by women and envied by men the world over.

The truth, however, was a far cry from his screen image. He was a homosexual, whose craving for taboo sex shattered forever his carefully crafted public persona and eventually cost him his life.

It was a secret that Rock had hoped to take to the grave with him. If it had not been for the effects of the disease, his wish might have been fulfilled.

Had it not been for the ravages of AIDS, Rock might have taken the secret of his homosexuality to the grave with him

But in the final weeks, not even he could hide the truth from outsiders any longer. His face was gaunt and ravaged. And his once strapping physique had been stripped to the bone.

But Rock did manage to hide the truth from most of the world - including his lover Marc Christian - for a full year.

It had begun as an irritation on his neck that refused to go away. But within a year, after going to a doctor in June

1984, Rock was stunned by the truth. It was the first sign of Kaposi's sarcoma, a cancer that afflicts AIDS patients.

Yet the star refused to reveal his affliction to anyone but his most trusted confidants, including his long-time secretary Mark Miller.

Two months after the diagnosis, the dying star travelled to France for the Deauville Film Festival and a retrospective of his life in films. On the advice of his Hollywood doctor, Rock stopped first in Paris to begin an experimental treatment course with the drug HPA-23.

But his desperate bid for a cure failed, and by November his appearance had altered dramatically. At his fifty-ninth birthday party, which Christian hosted at their Hollywood love nest, guests couldn't help but notice the dramatic change in Rock's appearance.

He was drawn and weary. 'I've been on a diet,' he explained.

THE GAY YOUNG STAR

Of course, the world would soon know that his excuse was a lie. But then lying came easy to Rock, even when he was known as Roy Fitzgerald, one-time truck driver, vacuum cleaner salesman and Navy veteran, who had left his home town of Winnetka, Illinois for a crack at the bright lights of Hollywood.

Rock had been an only child growing

up in the Depression, the son of a car mechanic who left his young family when Rock was a small child. Young Roy grew up with a mother he adored and a stepfather he did not.

Although a popular lad, he maintained few ties to the town after he departed for the Navy and, later, Hollywood. That was in 1946, and the lonely, would-be actor would stand outside the gates of the movie studios hoping to be discovered.

Eventually, of course, he was discovered - but not outside a film lot. The following year, the twenty-two-year-old hopeful had gravitated to the gay community of nearby Long Beach. It was through this close-knit homosexual circle that he met Henry Willson, the legendary talent scout for the David O. Selznick Studio.

According to Hollywood lore Willson, who was also a homosexual, renamed his latest discovery for the Rock of Gibraltar and the Hudson River.

After Hudson shot to stardom, he could not even be seen dining out with his gay partner for fear of scandal

---

From the very beginning of his career, Hudson projected one image in front of the camera and another away from it, and went to extreme lengths to cover up his homosexuality in public. He and his two best friends at the time, George Nader - another struggling actor - and Mark Miller even developed code words so they could talk freely in public.

The charade fooled the public, but those working with Rock knew his secret.

'We all knew Rock was gay, but it never made any difference to us,' recalled Mamie Van Doren, a sexy starlet who was one of many young actresses to go on arranged dates with Hudson.

By 1953, when Rock had already appeared in several films but had not yet climbed the rung to stardom, he met and fell madly in love with Jack Navaar. Even though the two soon moved in together, Hudson could never show any public affection for Navaar.

The ruse would take its toll on the affair, especially in 1954 when Rock starred in *Magnificent Obsession*, the film which made him a headline star.

Above: *Hudson with Sophia Loren and Ruth Leunerik at a German film awards ceremony in 1962.*

Right: *Sexy Italian star Gina Lollobrigida regularly starred opposite Rock Hudson. They are seen here throwing grapes during a Hollywood party.*

Now firmly in the public eye, the actor could no longer even go out to dinner with Navaar. Inevitably, the romance ended within twelve months.

To safeguard his reputation as an all-American film hunk, Rock did not live with another man for ten years.

Despite carefully crafted smoke screens, however, in 1955 the scandal sheet *Confidential* was rumoured to be preparing an expose on the star's taboo lifestyle. Instead, Universal made a deal with the magazine: it traded information on Hudson for dirt on a lesser-known actor - his friend George Nader.

A MARRIAGE OF CONVENIENCE

The brush with scandal, however, had been too close for the studio executives. In a bid to silence any further whispers about Rock's sexual orientation, they hastily arranged a wedding between him and his agent's secretary, Phyllis Gates.

The ceremony took place on 9 November and went ahead even though neither Rock nor the studio bothered to tell Gates that he was gay.

It wasn't until the very end of their marriage, which lasted almost three years, that she even discovered Rock was a homosexual. Years later, after the star's death, she would also recall that he sometimes beat her - probably out of his inner rage at the studio-organized scam.

For much of the 1960s he continued his lusty adventures unabated, taking numerous lovers. Thanks to loyal friends, there wasn't even a hint of scandal...until the early 1970s when a callous jokester almost damaged his career and reputation beyond repair.

Rock sometimes beat Phyllis, probably because he was furious that the studio had forced him into marriage

---

The malicious prankster had sent out wedding invitations, inviting several noted show business columnists to attend the 'marriage' of Rock and his good friend singer/actor Jim Nabors.

It was an unfounded hoax, and even though Hudson's career was not damaged Nabors wasn't so lucky. Soon afterwards his top-rating television variety series was cancelled.

Rock's superstar status, the fact that he did not flaunt his homosexual lifestyle in public and his reputation for being 'a good soldier' for the studio saved him when other gay actors floundered.

But the Nabors tragedy did take its toll psychologically, and Rock became even more paranoid about his gay lifestyle. He came to shun nights out on the town, preferring to entertain at his Beverly Hills estate, nicknamed 'The Castle'.

By the mid-1970s Rock was limiting most of his acting to the stage, until he was offered the lead role as Police Commissioner McMillan in *McMillan and Wife*. It was filmed in San Francisco, the so-called 'Gay Capital of America'.

Here, at last, Rock found a sanctuary. With his closest friends he frequented gay discos and bars, and revelled in the more liberal climate. He became more confident in his homosexuality, so much

so that some confidants urged him to tell the world he was gay.

But Hudson refused, for business as well as personal reasons. He believed that movie-goers weren't ready to imagine that their leading man often rode off into the sunset with another man.

Hudson felt movie-goers weren't ready to be told that their favourite leading man had his own favourite leading man

---

By this time Rock was living again with a lover - publicist Tom Clark. Clark was a far cry from the pretty-faced men he usually courted. But he enjoyed the same hobbies of football, cooking and travelling as Rock did, and became the great love of the star's life. For the first time ever, Hudson could now actually take a man with him anywhere he wished - Tom had become the actor's manager.

'I can even introduce him to Princess Margaret,' Rock once boasted to friends.

Below: *Rock Hudson and Claudia Cardinale starred in the 1965 movie* **Blindfold.** *She was one of a string of pretty actresses he made movie love to.*

Although Rock was deeply in love with Clark, that didn't stop him from having what he called 'beauties' parties'. A dozen or so of the couple's closest friends would be invited, as well as up to fifty stunning young men for orgies.

After over-indulgence with sex and alcohol, Hudson suddenly had to reassess his life when he needed heart by-pass surgery

---

By 1977, however, Rock began his four-year slide into near-oblivion. Worried about his age and faltering career, he took to the bottle. But in 1981 his wild lifestyle came to a sobering end. He had to have heart by-pass surgery.

The operation had another effect, recalled old friend George Nader: 'He woke up from the drunkenness of the 1970s. The meanness and sniping fell

Below: ***Live on stage...*** *Hudson and Juliet Prowse in* **I Do! I Do!** *a musical at London's Phoenix Theatre in 1975.*

Below right: ***Rock and Juliet at the first night party of*** **I Do! I Do!**

away, and he was returning to the Rock we had known in 1952 - a warm human being who laughed and played games.'

ENTER MARC CHRISTIAN

But the actor had grown tired of Tom Clark, and the year after his operation began his last serious affair. The object of his affection was a younger, more virile man, Marc Christian.

Rock had met the twenty-nine-year-old Marc in October 1982 at a charity do in Los Angeles. 'I gave him my phone number, but he didn't call for three weeks,' Christian recalled years later. 'Finally he asked me out on a date. That date led to another. He was a true gentleman - it took quite a few dates before he even tried to kiss me.'

But early in the spring of 1985, Christian's good life came to an end. Hudson began to see less of him, as constant battles with flu and fatigue kept the actor frequently bedridden.

He had been diagnosed as having AIDS a year earlier, but Marc was left in the dark. 'That's when Rock began to lead a true double life,' said Christian.

Although Hudson's appearance began to change - he became dramatically thin - his appeal as a leading man did not. *Dynasty* creator Esther Shapiro successfully approached him to join the cast of the soap opera as a love interest for Linda Evans' character, Krystle.

But even when he did that now-famous scene in which he kissed Evans, Hudson refused to tell her he had AIDS.

In July 1985 Rock flew to Paris for more treatments, but he passed out in his

about Rock's disease until 'I heard it on the 6 o'clock news', was not allowed in to see him because Mark Miller had compiled a visitors' roster without his name on it.

But a few days later Marc confronted Miller in person and was finally given permission to see his ailing lover.

His lover Marc Christian was not allowed to see Rock in hospital

---

Marc recalled:

I asked him, 'Why didn't you tell me you had AIDS?' He avoided giving me a direct answer. There is no answer to that question. He said, 'When you have this disease, you're all alone.' I told him, 'You're wrong. You know that if you'd told me you had AIDS, I'd have helped you to get treatment...' He just looked at the wall and didn't say anything.

Eventually Rock went home...there was nothing doctors could do for him. When he could, he would take short walks beside his pool.

Although he had been raised a Catholic, Rock had let his religious beliefs slip. But on 25 September, a priest visited him at the estate.

The star made his confession and received Communion. Then he was administered the last rites. His once-strapping frame was deathly thin and covered with lesions and bed sores.

The day before he died, Elizabeth Taylor paid a visit, but Rock, who was being fed from an intravenous drip, was slipping into a coma.

The following morning, Rock awoke early and was dressed by a nurse. But Clark, who had returned to the estate to watch over his dying friend, didn't think Rock was well enough to get up. So he undressed him and put him back in bed.

Some thirty minutes later, Rock Hudson was dead.

WHAT PRICE LOYALTY?

But his greatest dread, that his fans would desert him once they knew the shocking truth, never did come to pass. Instead, they responded to his plight with sympathy, and a curiosity about this still-

suite at the Ritz Hotel. Finally, it was decided that Rock was too weak even to undergo another AIDS treatment, so the actor decided to return to Los Angeles. But before he did, it was at last announced to the world, on 25 July, that the ageing heart-throb had AIDS. The decision finally to tell the truth, confidants recalled, was Hudson's alone.

'The hardest thing I ever had to do in my life was to walk into his room and read him the press release,' said one of them. 'I'll never forget the look on his face...In his eyes was the realization that he was destroying his own image.'

When Hudson returned to Los Angeles, he came in the middle of the night aboard a chartered 747 jet from which he was removed on a stretcher. He was transferred by helicopter to hospital, where a procession of close friends, including Elizabeth Taylor, Carol Burnett and Tony Perkins later came to visit him.

Yet Christian, who had not known

Above: A moustached Hudson takes a break during the filming in Italy of Il Vespaio - The Wasps Nest.

Above: *Period piece...*
Elizabeth Taylor and Kim
Novak were Hudson's co-
stars in **The Mirror**
Crack'd *made in 1981.*

mysterious disease. On the day he died, the US House of Representatives passed a bill allocating almost $200 million for AIDS research in the following year. And Elizabeth Taylor galvanized Hollywood and the world into action with her plea: 'Please God, he did not die in vain.'

Rock's death at last made AIDS a front-page issue around the world

---

Of course, he did not. The revelation of his illness did much to spur on the fight against AIDS, as the disease finally moved to the front pages of newspapers around the globe.

That all meant little to Christian, however, who received nothing in the actor's will. Reportedly, Rock left the bulk of his estimated $27 million estate to Miller and George Nader.

But later that year Marc filed a claim against Rock's estate, saying he 'would not have risked death by continuing to engage in sexual relations with Hudson' had he known about the disease.

His attorney, famed divorce lawyer Marvin Mitchelson, categorized it as 'the most unpleasant lawsuit I've ever been involved with.'

In February 1989 a jury ruled that Rock was in fact guilty of 'outrageous conduct' for concealing his AIDS diagnosis from Christian, although he did not contract AIDS. Hudson's estate appealed, but in June 1991, an appeals court upheld his $5 million award.

Despite the rancour surrounding his final days, Rock Hudson is still considered one of Hollywood's brightest lights. His public, the fans he thought he could not trust with his deepest secret, remain as loyal to his memory as they were before. Rock had underestimated them - but they forgave him for that, too.